Art Inspired by
Different Cultu

Lilian Coppock

Acknowledgements

The author would like to thank the children and staff of Dunbury First School for their contributions to this book, especially Felicity Stebbings for the batik on page 11, and Mary Nicholson for the African stencil work on page 15. Thank you also to Ruth Lancaster of Orleans Infant School for contributing her adinkra feltwork on page 14.

Grateful thanks to Gill Osborne for supplies of sheep's fleece, to Tomoko Murakami for help and suggestions on Japanese art work, and to the Ethnography Department of the British Museum for their helpful advice.

Finally, a big thank you to the children of Quarleston Farm art group – Juliet, Ben, Hamish, Charlotte, Emily, Bridie, Joshua and Jack (aged 6 to 11) – for their enthusiastic interest in the art of other cultures.

Decorated felt hangings (page 9)

African geometric masks (page 69)

Published by Collins, An imprint of HarperCollins*Publishers*
77 – 85 Fulham Palace Road, Hammersmith, London, W6 8JB

Browse the complete Collins catalogue at
www.collinseducation.com

© HarperCollins*Publishers* Limited 2011
Previously published in 2005 by Folens as 'Art of Different Cultures'
First published in 2000 by Belair Publications

10 9 8 7 6 5 4 3 2 1

ISBN-13 978-0-00-743943-0

British Library Cataloguing in Publication Data
A Catalogue record for this publication is available from the British Library

Every effort has been made to trace copyright holders and to obtain their permission for the use of copyright material. The authors and publishers will gladly receive any information enabling them to rectify any error or omission in subsequent editions.

Editors: Elizabeth Miles/Nina Randall   Cover design: Mount Deluxe
Page Layout: Suzanne Ward   Photography: Kelvin Freeman

Printed and bound by Printing Express Limited, Hong Kong

Mixed Sources
Product group from well-managed forests and other controlled sources
www.fsc.org   Cert no. SW-COC-001806
© 1996 Forest Stewardship Council

FSC

Contents

Introduction

Textiles, drawing, painting and sculptural forms have been integral to the lifestyles and beliefs of many cultures, since the earliest cave paintings of our ancestors. The world's different cultural groups have a huge diversity of styles, designs, materials and techniques in their arts and crafts, and these vary not only between one culture and another, but even between different villages.

It is fascinating, however, to see that widely separated cultures sometimes share common patterns, colours and forms. For instance, the decorative cross-hatching and animal images in Aboriginal paintings of Arnhem Land have much in common with the textured animals and patterns on Ashanti designs from Ghana.

Today's craft traditions are not rigidly bound to the past, but are continuously evolving. Old designs are passed on to the next generation, but many are lost, then reinvented and interpreted in a different way. Craft producers may adapt colours, motifs or decoration to suit market demands. A traditional floor covering may be sold as a wall-hanging or bedcover; an African winnowing basket may be sold as a tray; or a sand painting may be interpreted in paint or textiles.

Developing children's appreciation of the art of other cultures is a rewarding and worthwhile objective. It is a unique way to link Art and Humanities: colour, texture, pattern, shape and form become directly relevant to History, Geography, religious customs and lifestyles. Looking at similarities and differences in craft traditions will help to develop visual perception, critical observation, imagination, open-mindedness and understanding.

A sensitive introduction to lifestyles other than the children's own will also contribute to the development of tolerance and appreciation of others' beliefs.

This book has been arranged into the four main curricular areas of Art: textiles, drawing, painting and three-dimensional work. Many craft traditions adapt easily from one medium to another – for instance, those of printing, embroidery and collage work. Many of the crafts are also adaptable according to the age of the children.

I hope the children enjoy experimenting, developing and interpreting the motifs, patterns and forms in their own way.

Lilian Coppock

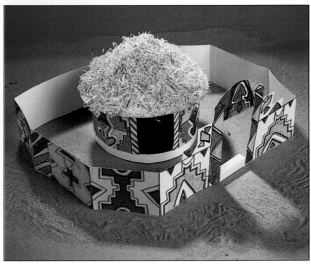

⚠ Some of the activities in this book will need careful supervision to ensure, for example, the safe use of dyes, bleaches, hot irons, hot wax and craft knives. Protect clothes and work surfaces where appropriate. Spray-paint and fixative sprays should be used in a well-ventilated area, and hands should be thoroughly washed after handling raw fleece, salt dough or dyes.

Spinning Wool

Simple threads for weaving can be made by rolling wool fibres between the palms or against the thigh, a method still practised in parts of Asia and Africa.

Resources
- Raw sheep's fleece in natural colours
- Neutral coloured wool and felts
- Card loom (see picture, below)
- Card shuttles (see photograph right)

Alpaca Weaving, Bolivia

Approach

1. Wind up a square loom with 18 warp threads, using bought wool for strength.

2. Take a small handful of fleece. Tease and separate the fibres, then stroke them in the same direction.

3. Pull out an end of the teased fleece with the left hand and roll the fibres down the thigh with the right palm to form a thread. Gently stretch and roll in the same direction. Uneven and fluffy bits will add to the texture.

4. Weave short lengths of the threads in and out of the prepared warp, leaving the ends loose at the sides. Build up rows of neutral threads to make a background. Push the rows together and roughly trim at the sides.

5. Cut the warp threads at the back, remove the card and tape down the warp ends.

6. Cut out an alpaca (llama) from felt and glue or stitch it to the weaving.

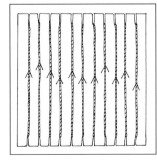

Card loom and warp threads

Zigzag Design, Ecuador

Approach

1. Prepare a rectangular loom with ten warp threads using thick, bought wool.

2. Prepare two shuttles, one with brown wool, one with a neutral colour. To do this, tease and roll a long thread (as above) and tie it to the shuttle. Add teased wool to the end of the thread by rolling the ends together, always twisting in the same direction. As it is spun, wind the thread round the shuttle until full.

3. Weave the design, passing the shuttle under and over the warp. Weave brown wool over ten warp threads on the first row, nine on the second and so on, to make a brown zigzag. Then work a white zigzag to complete the weaving. Cut the warp threads at the back, remove the card and tie the threads in pairs. Add extra fluffy wool bits to the fringe, if desired.

Wool Winding

Ethiopian Rug

Many African rugs are made from undyed hand-spun wool. The fleece colour of Ethiopian rugs varies from creamy white to dark brown.

Resources

- Wool in natural colours
- Piece of neutral cloth
- Oddments of felt and card
- Handful of raw wool
- Double-sided adhesive tape

Approach

1. Design your hanging on paper, using motifs such as the Ethiopian cross, lions, birds, churches, triangles and diamonds. Choose which motifs are to be wrapped with wool. Draw these on card and cut them out. Draw and cut out from felt the motifs you wish to glue or stitch on.

2. To wrap a card motif, put double-sided adhesive tape around the corners to hold the wool. Wind wool round and round the card, keeping the strands close together and fairly tight. Tuck loose ends into the back. The cross in the photograph was made in two pieces, and glued at the centre.

3. Glue all the card-wrapped and felt motifs to the backing cloth and fringe the two sides.

4. To finish the top and bottom edges, cut card strips to the correct length. Lie fluffy oddments of raw wool along the card and attach it by winding wool loosely around the raw wool and card. Glue the card strips in place.

Mexican Hanging

The Huichol people of Mexico wear clothes with colour codes that date back to the ancient Maya civilisation: blue (water); green (renewal, and the centre of the Earth); and white, yellow, red and black (North, South, East and West).

Resources

- Ring of stiff card, 20cm in diameter
- White, yellow, red, black wool for winding
- Green wool for warp threads
- Chunky wool in blue for the weft
- Teased raw wool dyed blue
- Feathers

Approach

1. Mark the card ring into four equal sections for the colours shown in the photograph.

2. Attach eight or nine green warp threads from the white to the yellow section. Tie or tape these in place.

3. Wind coloured wool tightly around each section to represent North, South, East and West. Cover the knots or tape at the warp ends.
   Overlap the ends to add new lengths of wool, tucking the last end into the back.

4. Weave blue wools in and out of the weft threads. Work in short lengths of rolled raw wool for extra texture.

5. Trim the sides of the weft ends and glue on a few decorative feathers.

Ikat Weaving

Ikat is an ancient craft in Indonesia, Thailand and other parts of Southeast Asia. Warp threads are tied and dyed and then woven to produce an exact pattern. In Sabu Island, Indonesia, patterns on men's clothes include stars, diamonds and zigzags; women's patterns include butterflies, birds and animals. The Ikat method has been adapted here to make pieces of weaving for a hanging, a pot cover and a small bag.

Resources
- White cotton yarn or string
- Cold water dyes or natural dyes
- Plastic carrier bags cut into 3cm strips
- Notched card looms
- Coloured felt
- Plastic pot

Approach

Bound yarn

1. Wind 8 to 10m of yarn into a long skein around the back of a chair. Lay the skein on a worktop and bind it up with plastic strips, as tightly as possible (see drawing). The bound areas will resist the dye.

2. Immerse the tied yarn in dye for the specified time, remove and allow to dry. If a two-colour effect is required, such as for the pot cover, dye the yarn in the lighter colour before binding. When dry, bind and immerse in the second dye colour. Cut off all the plastic strips and roll the yarn into a ball.

3. Wind up a card loom with warp threads. Use a long, narrow loom for the bag and pot cover.

4. Weave the weft threads in and out of the warp threads, taking care not to pull the edges tightly so that the weaving stays an even width. Push the rows together and tuck new ends behind the work. Continue until the weaving is long enough. To weave a diamond, draw a symmetrical diamond on paper and slide it behind the warp threads. Work rows of threads to cover the diamond. Then work rows of undyed thread for the background, joining it up to the diamond so that there are no gaps.

5. Cut the warp threads at the back, remove the card loom and tie the warp threads together in pairs. Glue the hangings to a piece of felt, and glue on a felt Sabu shape if desired, such as a star or bird. For details of the butterfly, see page 9. Glue the pot cover round a plastic pot, tucking in all the ends. Fold the bag weaving in half, stitch up the sides and sew on a plaited handle.

 Clothing should be well protected and rubber gloves should be worn.

Asian Felt

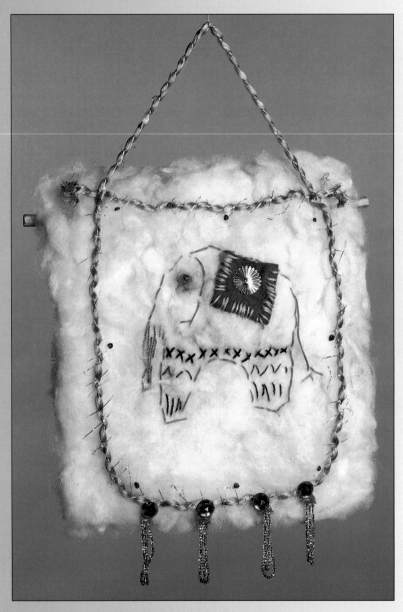

Felt has been made for many centuries in a wide belt of Asian countries from Turkey, through Central Asia to Mongolia and Siberia. Turkomen women make felt into carpets and saddle bags. Asian nomads make it into warm capes, hats and coats. In Mongolia, huge pieces of felt are stretched over a wooden frame to make circular tents called yurts, which repel the rain but allow light in and smoke out.

Resources
- Raw wool, teased and cleaned (see page 5)
- 0.75m² of net curtain
- Newspapers
- Soap and hot water
- Hairbrushes

Approach

1. Lay fluffy pieces of teased wool in the centre of the netting, arranging the fibres horizontally into a square shape. Two hairbrushes can be used to fluff up and stroke the fibres, a small handful at a time. Then add another layer, arranging the fibres vertically, then another horizontally. Build up the layers until about 5cm high.

2. Fold the netting over the wool to make a flat, square package, and then turn it over.

3. Lie the package on a thick layer of newspaper and rub the top of the netting with soap and hot water, working on a small area at a time. Press and rub gently in a circular motion, keeping the package square. Turn it over and repeat.

4. Roll up the package, rinse well to remove the soap, and squeeze out the water without wringing. Unroll, and remove the felt. Allow to dry before stitching.

Indian Namdha

Namdha rugs are made with undyed felt in Kashmir, in the Himalayas. They are embroidered with motifs, such as elephants, tigers, peacocks, flowers and trees.

Resources
- Handmade felt (see instructions above)
- Braid, felt, sequins, tassels
- Coloured threads
- Neutral backing cloth

Approach

1. Draw a motif on paper. Cut it out and pin it to the felt.

2. Stitch around the paper outline as closely as possible with backstitch or whipped running stitch, and remove the paper.

3. Design some stitch patterns on the paper, such as crosses, lines or zigzags. Sew your design on the felt in bright colours.

4. Finish by stitching on a braid border, felt details, tassels and sequins.

5. Stick or sew the handmade felt to a piece of backing cloth, so the work can be hung without stretching.

Decorated Felt Hangings

Felt rugs and hangings were greatly valued across Asia for thousands of years. Felt hangings with appliquéd designs lined the tombs of Siberian tribal chiefs, and rugs decorated with flowers, birds and animals were given as gifts to the Chinese royal court.

Sheep's wool can be dyed to make attractive felt backgrounds for stitching and collage work. The natural lanolin in fleece will repel dye if it is not carefully hand-washed. Immerse the fleece in tepid water overnight, drain it without heavy squeezing, then drop it into soapy water. Gently move it round but do not rub. Rinse in tepid water and dry on a rack.

Many materials can be stitched to a felt background. Try palm-spun threads, glittery threads, ribbons, oddments of chiffon or twisted net, dried flowers, feathers, beads and sequins.

Resources
- Felt-making materials (see page 8)
- Oddments for decorating the felt (see above)
- Natural or cold water dyes

 Clothing should be well protected and rubber gloves should be worn.

Approach

1. Wash the prepared raw wool as above. Dye small quantities in a range of colours to suit a theme, such as autumn, snow, fire, jungle or sunset. Shown above is a sky background with white, blue and purple wool. Below is a sea background with blue, green, yellow, white and purple wool.

2. Arrange the chosen colours of dyed wool on some net curtain and make a felt square as on page 8.

3. Decorate the felt square. Simple shapes such as a fish (below left) can be made from a soaped handful of fleece, flattened and shaped. Other soaped oddments could include leaves, seaweed or flowers. A soaped felt circle can be used to make a spider, snail, sun or hot-air balloon (see page 2). Little soaped balls of felt in several colours can be cut in half when dry to reveal the coloured layers inside (see the tiny fish, below left). Dried felt shapes can be decorated with stitches and beads, then sewn on a background. Glitter can be sprinkled into the felt.

4. To make the butterflies (above), fold a 7cm square of cotton cloth in half and drop coloured dyes onto it. Unfold the cloth and cut out a butterfly shape incorporating the symmetrical colours.

Egyptian Cartouche in Batik

The ancient Egyptians invented a system of picture writing called hieroglyphics, which represented words or sounds. A cartouche is an oval-shaped emblem of papyrus or stone with the name of a king or queen of Egypt inscribed in hieroglyphs.

Resources
- White cotton cloth
- Coloured fabric dyes
- Wax pot and brushes
- Sequins and glitter
- Clothes iron
- Newspaper

Approach

1. Design your cartouche on paper. Decide whether to include your whole name or just your initials, and add any numbers that are significant to you, such as your age. Keep each hieroglyph large and well-spaced.

2. Draw the design very lightly in pencil on the cloth. Paint over the shapes in the design with a brush dipped in melted wax.

3. Paint prepared dyes over the cloth, using a clean brush for each colour.

4. When dry, iron between several changes of newspaper, until all the wax is removed.

5. Decorate further with sequins, glitter or stitching.

6. Cut the design into an oval shape and mount on gold paper.

⚠ **Careful adult supervision is necessary for activities involving hot wax, hot irons and dyes. Clothing and work surfaces should be well protected.**

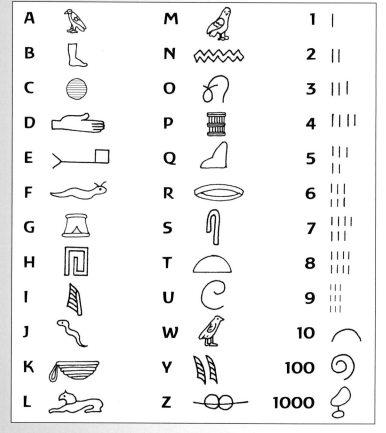

Hieroglyphs: alphabet and numbers

Personalised Batik

Batik is a craft from Indonesia. It involves covering areas of cloth with hot melted wax, which resists the application of coloured dyes. The traditional patterns used on the robes of early Javanese kings are today made up into sarongs and skirt pieces. The finely drawn, complex designs include flowers, birds and animals.

Resources
- Squares of cotton cloth
- Coloured fabric dyes
- Wax pot and tjantings
- Stitching materials, beads, sequins, buttons

Approach

1. Plan the composition carefully on paper, including images that are important to the child, such as people, pets and holidays. When complete, lightly outline the composition on the cloth in pencil.

2. Fill a tjanting with melted wax and practise using it on newspaper to find out how to make lines and spots. A fine tjanting gives good drips and spots. A thick tjanting needs to be moved quite quickly to give an even line.

3. After practising, refill a tjanting, holding a scrap of newspaper under the spout to catch drips and to transfer wax from the pot to the cloth. Begin by drawing wax lines over the pencil lines on the cloth. When complete, paint on, or dip the cloth into, the lightest colour of dye.

4. Allow to dry before applying more wax details such as patterns, lines and spots. Paint on a second, darker colour of dye, either all over the cloth, or on selected areas.

5. Dry off and repeat until the cloth has had three or four applications of wax and dye colours. The cloth may be crunched up after each waxing, to give a typical Indonesian cracked effect. The edges of the cloth can be dipped in a very dark dye to give a border effect.

6. Iron off all the wax between several changes of newspaper.

7. Embellish further with a little stitching, or a few beads, buttons and sequins.

 Careful adult supervision is necessary for activities involving hot wax, hot irons and dyes.

Australian Aboriginal Images in Batik

Australian Aboriginal tradition says that Dreamtime was when ancestral beings (people, animals, birds, plants, rain, clouds and stars) moved on the Earth. The ancestors gave the people laws on how to live together and how to live on the land without harming it. Knowledge of the Dreamtime is kept alive in song, ceremony, learning and art works such as sand paintings.

The theme for this batik piece is the Aboriginal hunter and the food that might be hunted or gathered. Typical animal images include the kangaroo, long-necked turtle, snake, fish, crocodile, iguana and birds. Elements of desert art are also incorporated: dots, repeated marks and concentric circles and patterns.

Resources
- Large piece of white cotton cloth
- Fabric dyes (red, browns, yellows, black)
- Clothes iron
- Wax pot and tjantings
- Paintbrushes

Approach

1. Use a pencil to divide the cloth into areas, one for each child. Alternatively, each child can complete a separate oblong of batik and these can be stitched together when complete. Each child draws a chosen design in pencil on their area – an animal, plant, person, trees or designs representing waterholes, stars or pathways across the land (see page 42).

2. Practise using a tjanting, as on previous page, and apply wax lines over the pencil lines. Next, draw wax patterns on the animals' bodies, and in background areas include lots of spots, lines and circles.

3. When all the areas have been waxed, paint dyes onto the designs, using thick brushes for background areas and fine ones for details. Dyes can be mixed and contrasting spots of colour can be dropped onto background areas.

4. A second application of spots or lines of wax may be added when the dye is dry using fine brushes, followed by a different colour of dye on top.

5. Iron off all the wax between changes of newspaper.

 Careful adult supervision is necessary for activities involving hot wax, hot irons and dyes.

Stained Glass Window on Silk

The art of stained glass flowered in the Middle Ages in Europe, in Christian churches and cathedrals. Sometimes real jewels were inserted into the glass. The tradition of depicting Bible stories, saints, angels, heroes, demons and scenes of everyday life continues today in modern stained-glass masterpieces.

Resources
- Paper
- Piece of washed silk
- Silk paints and black gutta
- Adhesive tape
- Picture frame or cardboard carton

Approach

1. Cut the paper so that it is slightly smaller than the silk. Mark out an arched, circular or rectangular window shape on the paper. Choose a scene, such as a Bible story, and draw it on the paper in thick pencil.

2. Tape the drawing onto the work surface so that it will not move. Place the silk on top so that the drawing shows through, and tape the silk in place, too. Lightly trace over the pencil design onto the silk.

3. Either staple the silk to a wooden frame, or across the top of an open carton, so the silk is taut and does not touch the work surface. Trace over all the lines on the silk with black gutta, ensuring there are no gaps.

4. When the gutta is dry, gently paint colour onto the design. Touch the centre of each area with the brush – the paint will travel by itself but be stopped by the gutta. Experiment with colour mixing by dropping on different colours, adding water for lighter colours or more paint for darker colours. Use a clean brush for each colour.

5. When dry, remove the silk and mount in a black frame. Glue on sequins for extra richness.

Minoan Fresco on Silk

The great Minoan palaces of Crete abounded with brilliantly coloured wall paintings such as the surviving 'Bluebird' and 'Bull – Leaping Sport', painted 4000 years ago. As an island people, the Minoans were particularly attracted to the sea and its creatures.

Working as described above, draw a Minoan scene of birds, animals or sea creatures on the silk. Sprinkle rock salt on the wet background for a speckled effect. Glue blue paper seahorse heads onto strips of white card for a border.

Adinkra Printed Cloth

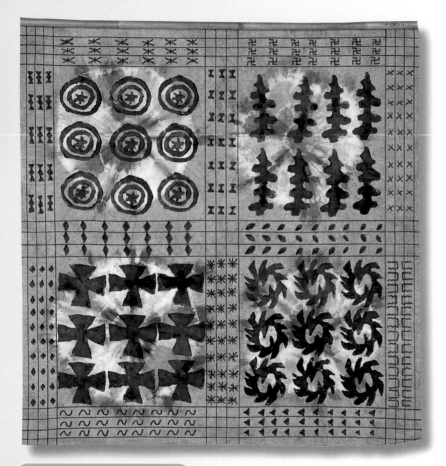

Adinkra means 'goodbye' to the Ashanti, and dark brown or red adinkra cloth is traditionally worn at funerals or when guests depart. Neutral or bright colours are worn for festive occasions.

Black symbols are stamped onto the dyed cloth, using calabash shell printing blocks. More than fifty symbols exist, each with a mystical meaning. A motif is repeat-printed in each square. Shown left, clockwise, are Ananse the spider (top left), courage, unity and good fortune. Others are shown in the photographs below (for example, a five-pointed star for Child of the Sky, three concentric circles for the King and a crescent below a wheel shape for faithfulness).

Resources
- White cotton cloth
- Coloured dyes (e.g. blue for celebration)
- Black fabric paint and fabric pen
- Card, felt and wire
- Clothes iron

Approach

1. For each child or group, mark out in thick pencil a 20cm square with a 5cm border on the cloth.

2. Either dip the cloth into one pot of dye or tie-dye each square. To tie-dye, hold the centre of a square and bind wire round the cloth in three places, before dipping in several colours of dye. Allow to dry and iron flat.

3. Make a printing block by drawing and cutting a symbol from felt and gluing it to card. Glue a card handle to the back. Paint fabric paint onto the block and print rows of the pattern on each square.

4. Finish by drawing four lines with fabric pen to surround each of the squares. Additional repeat patterns can be drawn inside the lines.

 Careful adult supervision is necessary for activities involving hot wax, hot irons and dyes.

Adinkra Felt Work

Draw each symbol with chalk on black felt, and cut them out. Then pin each symbol to a white square and stitch it into place. Glue or stitch all the squares to a backing cloth for display.

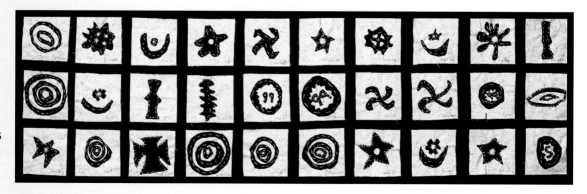

African Paste-resist Cloth

The application of starch paste to cloth as a method of dye-resistance is practised in many countries, including Africa, Japan and China. The Yoruba people of Nigeria produce blue patterned 'adire' cloth, using cassava flour and indigo dye, with stencils or hand printing.

Resources
- Flour-and-water paste
- Washing-up liquid container
- Square and rectangular pieces of white cotton cloth
- Dark blue fabric dye
- Wide-toothed comb

Approach

Method for Adire Squares

1. Mix some paste to a smooth, runny consistency and pour it into the container.

2. Draw, in drizzled lines, your chosen pattern on a square piece of cloth. Choose from birds, animals, flowers, leaves, stars or geometric patterns. Dry flat, until the paste is hard.

3. Paint dye onto the cloth, wetting the paste as little as possible.

4. When dry, pick off the paste and mount the design on white card with a border of blue lines.

Method for Ivory Coast Combed Border Patterns

1. Mix some paste, as before. Tape a rectangular strip of cloth to a board and paint paste evenly all over.

2. Comb patterns into the paste and then dry flat.

3. Paint with dye. When dry, remove the paste by dipping the cloth in water to soften the paste, and scrape it off with a wallpaper scraper. Mount on card as above.

Note: The work of a whole class can be displayed as a patchwork grid, with a border of combed patterns.

⚠ **Clothing should be well protected and rubber gloves should be worn.**

African Stencilled Cloth

Resources
- Square metre of yellow cloth
- Sticky-backed plastic
- Fabric paints and rollers
- Masking tape
- Clothes iron

Approach

1. Stick a border of masking tape to the cloth, 5cm in from the edges.

2. Draw your chosen images (sun, trees, elephant, cheetah, giraffe, antelope and snake) on the paper backing of the plastic. Cut them out and cut holes for eyes, spots or stripes.

3. Peel off the backing and arrange the images on the cloth.

4. Roll several colours of fabric paint all over the cloth.

5. When dry, peel off the plastic shapes and tape, and iron the cloth on the back to fix the colour. Use as a display cloth or cushion cover.

Nigerian Appliqué Design

In Nigeria, all kinds of items may be stitched onto cloth to indicate a person of importance. This design (left) is based on a Nigerian cushion of red leather, printed with black geometric patterns and animal forms.

Resources
- Red cloth
- Oddments of black felt, beads
- Black braid
- Black fabric pen or crayon

Approach

1. Draw a square centrally on the red cloth and stitch braid around it.

2. Divide the square by drawing a grid of nine smaller squares. Go over the drawn lines with whipped running stitch.

3. Draw geometric patterns in each small square, using fabric pen.

4. Cut out two different animal templates from card. Use these to cut out four of each animal from black felt. Pin and sew the animals around the central square.

5. Finish with small beads for the animals' eyes and a black felt fringe for the border.

Colombian Reverse Appliqué

This technique involves applying layers of cloth to a backing and then cutting away shapes to reveal the contrasting colours beneath. Reverse appliqué is worked by the Cuna people of Panama and Colombia. Motifs of birds, plants and animals are believed to give protection from evil spirits.

Resources
- 20cm squares of red and yellow felt
- 20cm square of brightly patterned fabric

Approach

1. Pin the three squares of cloth on top of each other at the corners, with the patterned fabric at the bottom.

2. On the top layer, draw a bird, person, plant or animal. Sew over the lines with whipped running stitch, through all three layers of cloth.

3. Use sharp pointed scissors to cut away the felt around the stitching, through the top layer only. Take care not to cut the stitches.

4. Cut out peephole geometric shapes inside the motif. Cut more peepholes through the middle layer of felt to reveal the bright pattern beneath.

5. Glue or stitch the two bottom layers together all around the edges. Mount on black card.

Indian Mango Designs

The mango motif, sometimes called the 'peacock', has been popular on the Indian subcontinent for hundreds of years. In Europe it is known as the Paisley pattern, after the Scottish town where it was imitated and printed onto cloth.

Resources

- Neutral cloth, coloured cloth, felt
- Fabric paints, gold paint
- Sticky paper labels
- Sequins
- PVA glue
- Scraps of lace
- Decorative oddments
- Glitter glue
- Clothes iron

Approach

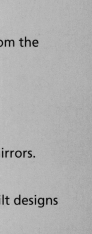

Method for Fabric with Painted Transfers (top left)

1. Draw four identical mango shapes on sticky paper labels and cut out. Then cut out a spiky shape from the centre of each. Peel off the backing and stick in a pattern on neutral cloth.
2. Roll several colours of fabric paint over the cloth. When dry, peel off the labels.
3. Iron on the reverse to fix the colours. Stitch on beads and curtain hooks for decoration.

Method for Felt Work with 'Mirrors' (top right)

1. Make paper patterns for mango shapes of different sizes. Pin the patterns to felt and cut them out.
2. Pin two mango felt shapes to the cloth and stitch them down. Glue on large and small sequins as mirrors.

Method for Kantha-style Fabric (bottom left)

1. Using fabric paint, draw a mango shape onto neutral cloth, with a design inside. Typical Kantha quilt designs from Bangladesh include lotus flowers, leaves, birds, fish and animals.
2. When dry, iron on the reverse to fix the colour.
3. Embellish with stitching and dots of fabric glitter.

Method for Block-printed Diwali Cloth (bottom right)

1. Make a printing block by cutting a mango shape from card and gluing a lace flower centrally.
2. Paint the block with gold paint, and print four mangoes symmetrically on the cloth.
3. When dry, glue on gold oddments (ribbon, sequins and pipe-cleaners).

Block-printed Borders

All the work above has borders of card, printed with a block dipped in paint. The blocks were made as follows.

Painted Transfers:	Mould Plasticine into a flat mango shape, dip in silver paint and print.
Felt Work:	Cut a mango shape from polystyrene, dip in silver paint and print.
Kantha Fabric:	Stick string onto card in a mango shape, paint on white paint and print.
Diwali Cloth:	Cut a mango shape from polystyrene, dip into PVA glue and print. Sprinkle on gold glitter.

Thai Stitching Patterns

The women of the hill tribes in the north of Thailand produce exquisite needlework designs. The cross-stitch designs on the boxes are adapted from Hmong tribe collar pieces. The star stitch design is a decoration from the indigo-dyed cloth of the Mien tribe, used on a waistcoat or turban edge. The Karen tribe weave a red and yellow striped cloth for sarongs, embroidered and decorated with seeds.

Resources

- Small square of binca
- Handmade card box with lid (see drawing)
- Graph paper (1cm squares)
- PVA glue
- Ribbons, seeds
- Yellow cloth

Cross-stitch Boxes

Approach

1. Draw a cross-stitch design on the graph paper 13 by 13 squares, using two or three colours. Start at the centre and work outwards.
2. Pencil the design onto the binca, then sew over it in cross stitch.
3. Trim the edges and glue the work to the lid of the box. The lid is slightly larger than the base and has four lengths of paper straws glued under it to hold it in place on the base.

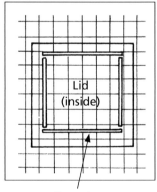

Lid (inside)

Paper straws

Method for Indigo Stars

1. Make a sewing card by stapling graph paper to a 12cm square of dark blue card at the corners. Push a needle through the paper and card at the grid junctions to create a 9 by 9 grid of holes.
2. Discard the graph paper. Stitch through the holes in the card to create two overlapping crosses to make a star.
3. Mount on a piece of fringed, dark blue cotton cloth, adding a border of whipped running stitch, if desired.

Method for Seed Stitching

1. Stitch two strips of red ribbon to a square of yellow cloth.
2. Arrange the seeds (such as melon, marrow and rosehip) in patterns in rows.
3. Stitch the seeds to the cloth, using a fine needle and thread.

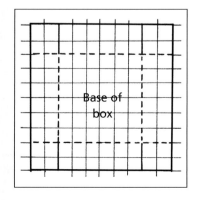

Base of box

Chinese Yin-Yang Hanging

The yin-yang is a symbol of the balance of opposites in nature. The eight trigrams on the hanging are symbols from mythology.

Resources
- 5 15cm squares of red felt
- 4 squares of white felt
- Oddments of red, black and white felt
- Glitter thread and fabric crayons
- White cotton backing-cloth

Approach

1. Measure and cut strips of felt to make the trigram patterns in the photograph. Pin the strips to a square of felt and stitch them down with glitter thread. Cross stitch is especially effective.

2. For the yin-yang, cut two circles 11.5cm in diameter in red and white felt. Draw the curving line across the white felt and cut along it. Pin and stitch the red and white yin-yang to a circle of black felt, 13cm in diameter. Glue the yin-yang to the central red felt square.

3. Assemble all the completed squares. Stitch or glue them in place.

4. Draw a thunderline design around the edges (see page 28) with black fabric pen and a bat in each corner. Fringe the edges and hang on bamboo.

Chinese Embroidered Purses

Traditionally, embroidered purses were given as presents at family celebrations. Typical motifs include good luck and long-life motifs such as the goldfish, phoenix and tortoise shown below, and various Chinese symbols (see page 29).

Resources
- 21cm square of felt
- Glittery ribbons and threads, beads
- Fabric glitter
- Oddments of fabric with fabric bonding applied to their backs

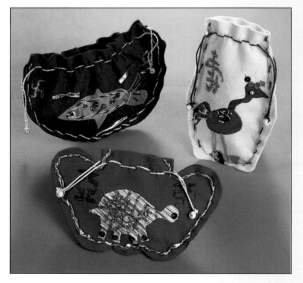

Approach

1. Make a paper template for your purse shape – traditional shapes are shown left (semi-circular, long hexagonal and ear-shaped). Cut two identical shapes from the felt square.

2. Draw a motif on the paper backing of the bonded fabric. Cut out the design and iron it onto one piece of felt. Embellish with stitches, oddments of ribbon and sequins.

3. Stitch the two pieces of felt together with whipped running stitch, leaving the top open.

4. Thread strong yarn across top edges so the purse can be closed. Tie beads to the ends of the yarn threads.

5. Paint on a good luck symbol using fabric glitter and leave the purse to dry.

Navajo Sand Paintings on Fabric

Sand painting is almost uniquely a Navajo art today. Ground-up pigments such as pollen, charcoal, sands and minerals are trickled through the fingers to make complicated patterns. Sand paintings are sometimes translated into the medium of textiles, as here.

Healing Chant

The figures in the photograph (left) are carrying symbols of the spirits of the sky: lightning, clouds, thunder and light rays. The central item is a stalk of maize – of great importance to the desert-living Navajo. The border is a long, striped human figure.

Approach

1. Sketch out a symmetrical design on thin paper, incorporating two or four figures.

2. Colour the design thickly with fabric crayons.

3. Iron the design onto the fabric. Protect the ironing board with newspaper under the fabric.

4. Embellish the design by drawing on extra details, outlines and patterns with felt-tipped fabric pens.

5. Fray the edges, hang from a dowel and glue on a few feathers.

Resources
- White polycotton cloth
- Fabric crayons
- Felt-tipped fabric pens
- Feathers
- Clothes iron
- Dowel

Mother Earth, Father Sky

Mother Earth and Father Sky are sacred figures from Navajo mythology. In this traditional design, sacred plants grow from Mother Earth; Father Sky is adorned with stars and the Milky Way, represented as a band of crosses.

Resources
- Frayed calico
- Brown fabrics or felts
- Felt oddments
- Glitter glue and sequins, sticky stars
- PVA glue

Approach

1. Draw and cut out a paper template of a figure. Cut two copies in brown fabrics and stitch or glue these to the calico.

2. Cut felt hands, feet and faces, and glue in place.

3. Embellish further with glitter glue to make the plant and Milky Way, add the stars, and any other details you wish.

20

Native American Quilling Designs

Plains Native Americans used quilling to embellish many items, such as bags, boxes, pouches, sheaths and clothing. Porcupine quills were dyed with natural colours and then pushed through holes in a piece of hide.

Resources
- Coloured plastic drinking straws
- White card
- Double-sided adhesive tape
- PVA glue
- Coloured felt, oddments of suede and fur

Approach

Method for Bag, Pouch and Knife Sheath

1. Cut two identical felt pieces to an appropriate shape for the yellow rectangular bag, the brown semicircular pouch or the long knife sheath. Stitch them together with blanket stitch or overstitch, leaving the top open. Cut fringes in the felt. Striped patterns in the fringes can be made by gluing on a contrasting felt strip before snipping the fringe. Add neck or belt loops of wool or suede.

2. Make a motif by cutting a simple design from card such as a rectangle or thunderbird to fit (see below).

3. Cover the card with double-sided adhesive tape. Cut lengths of straws and press them onto the tape; first make an outline with the straws, then fill with your chosen pattern and colours.

4. Glue the card design to your bag, pouch or sheath. Glue on any other decorative details you wish, such as oddments of fur or felt. Straws can be sewn directly onto the felt for additional decoration.

Method for Apache Collar

To make the Apache collar (top left in photograph), cut one piece of felt to the appropriate 'T' shape. Add a quilling design as described above, plus felt shapes. Thread lengths of straws onto wool for decoration. Add ribbon ties.

Method for Box

Adjust the card pattern on page 18 so that the base and lid are rectangular. Add a quill design to the lid as described above. Create patterns by colouring squared paper and glue onto the sides.

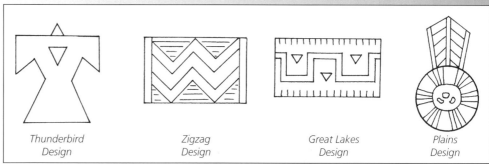

Thunderbird Design *Zigzag Design* *Great Lakes Design* *Plains Design*

Mexican Designs in Cross Stitch

These traditional designs are taken from Huichol beadwork bracelets. Traditional motifs used by Huichol people in Mexico have religious significance. Shown here are zigzag lines (for lightning or rain serpents), the double-headed eagle (the sky spirit) and the deer (the messenger of God).

Resources
- White oblong of binca
- Felt backing
- Coloured thread

Approach

1. Choose a design from those in the photograph on the left and mark it on the binca in pencil.

2. Follow the design in cross stitch. Use brightly coloured threads and work in a border of your choice around the edges.

3. Fray the edges and glue to a felt wristband. Add threads for tying.

Native American Basketry in Cross Stitch

Native American peoples make exquisite baskets, the designs of which lend themselves well to cross stitch.

Resources
- White binca dappled with yellow dye
- Graph paper
- Coloured thread

Approach

1. Show the children a range of pictures of basketry patterns before they begin. Human figures, faces and geometric patterns make good subjects for cross stitch.

2. Design a pattern on paper first, shading in the squares where crosses will be worked.

3. Mark the pattern on the binca in pencil and cover the pencil markings with cross stitches. Work a border round the edge.

Shown right are:

Top left: a standing figure from a Klikitat basket
Top centre: a stylised head from a Wasco woven bag
Top right: stepped oblong motifs from a Klikitat basket
Centre: geometric wave motif showing the importance of water, from a Pima basket
Bottom: a whale-hunting scene from a basketry hat woven by a Nootka chief.

Rock Art Pastel Drawings

Prehistoric art is often connected with initiation rites, ceremonial rituals or mythology. Rock art also portrays wild or domestic animals, hunting scenes or other aspects of daily life. The pastel drawings in the photograph are based on rock art from around the world.

Top left: Lascaux caves in France contain pictures of bulls, reindeer and horses painted by people who hunted this game. Some scenes show men wearing masks of the animals they hunted.

Top centre: Chinese rock painting of a warrior scene with swords, drums and a dog. The biggest rock painting in the world is at Huashan cliffs in China.

Top right: One of the well-known examples of X-ray style fish, showing the bones and intestines, from Arnhem Land, Australia.

Bottom left: Hunting scene with giraffe and elephant from Tanzania.

Bottom right: North American scene of goats and hunters.

Approach

Resources
- Sugar paper
- Chalk pastels
- Paints in muted colours
- Fixative
- Sponges

1. Look at a range of rock paintings from the culture being studied and choose a subject.

2. Sponge-print sugar paper with soft colours, blotting or adding water for a natural effect.

3. When the background is dry, draw the scene you have chosen in soft, natural-coloured pastels. Go over outlines, if necessary, with graphite pencil or felt-tipped pen. Spray with fixative.

Rock Art Etchings on Plaster

The above etchings on plaster were based on observational drawings of rock art from different cultures.

Top left: Tanzanian Trance Dance – five shamans, half human and half animal, in a ceremonial dance.

Top centre: Killer Whale and Faces – northwest coastal American depiction of whaling by the Makah tribe.

Top right: Tassili men with chariot – example of Sahara rock art with its rich details of clothes, everyday artefacts, cattle and hunting scenes.

Centre: She Who Watches – enormous northwest coastal American rock carving, thought to be a guarding spirit.

Bottom left: Californian Shaman – costumed and painted Shaman in a hunting ritual, wearing feathered headdress and bow and arrows.

Bottom centre: Doe and fawn – typical Indian geometric design in animal outlines.

Bottom right: Lightning Brothers – two huge figures with rayed headdresses and stone axes from Australian Aboriginal rock art.

Approach

1. Select a subject from a piece of rock art. Alternatively, design a drawing based on mythological beings or gods from a particular culture.

2. Smooth a piece of crumpled foil on a worktop and build an irregular wall of clay around it, 2cm high. Make sure there are no gaps.

3. Pour mixed plaster onto the foil until it is 1.5cm thick. Allow to set hard.

4. Peel off and discard the clay, and paint the rough underside of the cast in natural rock colours, sponging for a soft effect. Allow to dry.

5. Draw your design on the cast in pencil and scratch over the pencil lines with a pointed stick to reveal the light plaster beneath the paint.

Resources
- Plaster (see method on page 71)
- Muted paints
- Kitchen foil
- Sponges and pointed sticks
- Clay

Australian Aboriginal Rock Art

Wandjina Ancestral Beings

The Wandjina are ancestral beings from the sky and the sea, who bring the rains, and control the weather, fertility and all living things. Their faces and bodies are white. They have round black eyes and no mouth. The head often has a halo to represent hair or clouds, often with radiating lines for feathers or lightning. The lines of dots are similar to body painting designs.

Resources
- Earth-coloured sugar paper
- White chalk
- Black, white and ochre chalk pastels
- Fixative

Approach

1. Lightly pencil in the outlines of the figures on the sugar paper.

2. Holding a stick of white chalk on its side, rub chalk all over the body shapes. Smooth with a finger.

3. Outline the shapes in pastels, adding facial details, haloes and dots. Spray with fixative.

Rock Stencils

Stencilled art produced 10 000 years ago, in Queensland, shows hands, forearms, stone tools and different kinds of boomerang.

Resources
- Sponge-printed sugar paper (see page 23)
- Card
- Fixative
- Chalk pastels

Approach

1. Prepare card templates of children's hands or feet, and boomerangs and axes.

2. Arrange the card shapes on the prepared background and colour round each one thickly in pastels. Before removing the card, use a finger to smudge the pastel around the templates outwards.

3. Spray with fixative.

Egyptian Papyrus Drawings

Egyptian scribes wrote on elaborate papyrus scrolls. Papyrus reeds grow along the banks of the Nile. Strips of white pith from inside the stems were laid vertically and horizontally over each other. Heavy pressure and pounding with mallets released sap from the plant and bound the layers together. Sheets were joined to make a long scroll which could be rolled up.

Resources
- Rectangular sheet of paper
- Black graphite pencil
- Cellulose paste and large brush
- Felt-tipped pens or wax crayons
- Gauze bandages
- Gold fabric glitter

Approach

1. Paste a rectangular piece of paper with a large brush and lay strips of bandage neatly over it. Smooth them down and allow to dry.

2. Using a black graphite pencil, draw your chosen design on the 'papyrus'. The design might include gods, hieroglyphs, symbols, cartouches and kings (see page 10).

3. If desired, give the papyrus an aged look by adding a few cold-tea stains.

4. Test your felt-tipped pens on the bandage to make sure they will not spread and spoil the design before using them to apply colour. Wax crayons can also be used.

5. Highlight some areas with a little gold fabric glitter.

Note: The 'papyrus' can be made without using paper. To do this, lay strips of bandage closely alongside each other on a plastic bag. Paste more strips over the first layer, laying them in the opposite direction. Ensure there are no gaps between the layers.

Indian Mehndi Hand Patterns

In India, henna paste is used to draw intricate mehndi decorations on the hands, and sometimes the feet, of young women for special occasions such as weddings and festivals like Diwali. Mehndi signifies purity.

Resources
- Skin-coloured paper
- Discarded rubber glove for whole-hand cast
- Plaster (see recipe on page 71)
- Clay for hand plaque
- Red crayons, pastels or felt-tipped pens

Approach

Method for Paper Hands
1. Draw round your hand on the paper and cut out the hand shape.

2. Draw a pattern on it based on mango shapes (see page 17), large and small flowers, leafy tendrils and dots. Elaborate on the design as you work, keeping the same pattern for each finger.

Method for Whole-hand Cast
1. Mix some plaster (see method on page 71). Spoon it into the fingers of the glove, squeezing and tapping it down so that there are no air bubbles.

2. Fill the palm of the glove with plaster to 5cm from the top. Fold over the cuff and hang it up to dry for 24 hours.

3. Carefully cut off the glove bit by bit so the fingers do not break off. Decorate as above.

Method for Hand Plaque
1. Roll a slab of clay to a slightly larger size than your hand. Roll a fat sausage shape of clay and press it firmly all around the slab to make a low wall.

2. Press a hand into the clay, making as deep an impression as possible.

3. Fill the impression with plaster and leave to dry.

4. Peel off the clay and wash the cast. Paint and decorate when dry.

Variation
The footprint of Buddha, bearing eight symbols, was drawn in India to show the places He visited when preaching. The best known symbols are the wheel with eight spokes (symbol of the eight right steps to wisdom) and the lotus flower (symbol of His purity). Others include the endless knot, the parasol, the two goldfish and the canopy. Swastikas on the toes are an ancient Buddhist luck symbol.

Wheel

27

Chinese New Year Decorations

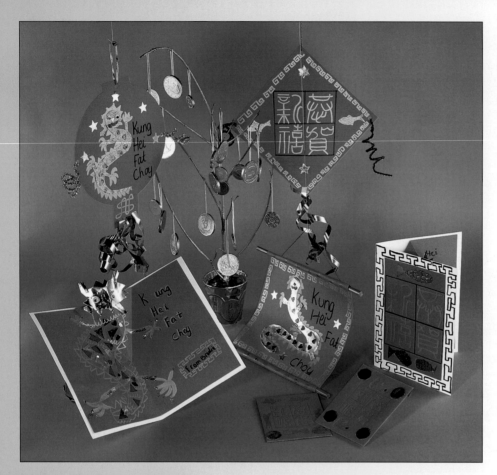

At Chinese New Year, red and gold good luck decorations are hung, children are given lucky money envelopes and coins are shaken from a money tree to bring good fortune. The decorations in the photograph were made for 2000, the Year of the Dragon. For other years, substitute the appropriate animal, for example, 2001 – Snake; 2002 – Horse; 2003 – Sheep.

Resources
- Flowerpot
- Plasticine
- Twig, painted gold
- Foil-covered chocolate coins
- Red and white card and paper
- PVA glue
- Red and gold foil
- Gold marker pen
- Red and gold oddments (glitter, sequins, ribbon, pipe-cleaners)
- Bamboo

Approach

Method for Money Tree
1. Cover a flowerpot with shiny papers, fill with Plasticine and push in a twig painted gold.
2. Hang foil-covered chocolate coins on it.

Method for Lucky Money Envelopes
1. Fold and glue red paper into a simple envelope.
2. Decorate with the words *Kung Hei Fat Choy* or use a gold marker pen to add Chinese calligraphy for Happy New Year in four squares (see top right hanging decoration in photograph).
3. Draw on goldfish (for abundance). Alternatively, glue on foil circle 'coins' made by rubbing a soft pencil over coins under gold foil.

Method for Hanging Decorations
1. Cut a circle or diamond from red card.
2. Decorate with thunderline (good luck) border patterns (see right), a gold decorated dragon, goldfish and Chinese greetings as above.
3. Add curled foil or pipe-cleaner streamers.

Method for Lucky Paper Scroll
1. Curl red paper round two pieces of bamboo.
2. Decorate as above.

Method for New Year Cards
1. Make a cover by folding a rectangle of white card in half. Decorate with New Year greetings and border patterns.
2. Make a pop-up inside by folding a sheet of red paper. Cut out a foil dragon's head and stick it down so that it projects above the card at the centre. Draw and decorate a dragon's body under the head on the red paper.
3. Glue the red pop-up dragon inside the white cover, ensuring no glue is applied to the triangular pop-up area.

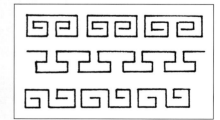

Thunderline designs

Chinese Blessings Cards

Resources
- White card
- Red felt
- Black sugar paper
- Red, black and gold felt-tipped pens

Lu pattern

Approach

1. Draw one of the large symbols, (right) on black sugar paper and cut it out. For the Riches symbol fold a circle into quarters and draw the shape shown in the drawing above. Cut away the white areas shown.

2. Go over the pencil lines with gold felt-tipped pen.

3. Glue the black symbol to a square of red felt and glue this to the front of the card.

4. Draw traditional motifs round the symbols in red, black and gold:

   Long Life (Shou): Peaches, tortoises and butterflies – symbols of long life.
   Good Luck (Wan): A traditional border pattern of mountains and waves (see drawing, right) can also be included.
   Happiness (Fu) Phoenixes – signs of goodness, which predict happy times.
   Riches (Lu): Bats – symbols of happiness.

Waves

Mountains

Clouds

Four Season Blossom Cards

Resources
- Oddments of fabric (white, yellow, pink, cerise) with fabric bonding applied to the back
- Blue paper border strips
- Blue silky cloth square for background
- Fabric pens and silver pen
- Folded sheet of white card
- PVA glue

Approach

1. Choose one of the following flowers and practise drawing it on paper, looking carefully at the petal shapes: peony for wealth – spring; lotus for purity – summer; chrysanthemum for friendship – autumn; cherry for beauty – winter.

2. Using fabric pens, draw the flower onto the bonded fabric. Cut it out, peel it off the backing and iron onto the blue cloth background square.

3. Using fabric pens, draw leaves, stems and stamens. Glue the square to the front of the card.

4. Glue four blue paper strips along the cloth edges and decorate them with a silver thunderline (see page 28).

5. Finish by writing on the meaning of the flower and the season.

Chinese Emperor Dragon Robe

In the fifteenth century, Chinese emperors wore resplendent silk robes, embroidered with 12 imperial symbols, chief of which was the dragon (symbol of heaven, king of the elements, god of water and bringer of rain).

Resources
- Paper for template
- Yellow satin cloth or yellow paper
- Fabric felt-tipped pens or T-shirt pens

Approach

Sun

Moon

Flaming Pearl

1. Draw and cut out a symmetrical template for the robe, as in the photograph above. Draw round this in pencil on the cloth. Also mark out a collar extending across the chest, a circle for the dragon and a border strip along the bottom.

2. Use fabric pens to draw a detailed dragon in the circle with a 'flaming pearl', symbolising the dragon's power over thunder and lightning (see right).

3. Fill in the border strip at the bottom with patterns of clouds for heaven, waves for seas and mountains for Earth (see page 29).

4. Draw Buddhist good luck symbols along the collar and strip across the chest.

5. Draw the 12 imperial symbols where you wish on the robe. The symbols in the photograph are as follows.

   Cuffs: Fu happiness symbol (see page 29).

   Shoulders: the sun (a phoenix in a red circle) for nobility (see right); a blue moon, with a hare preparing the elixir of life (see right); stars – the three circles symbolise the unity of the sun, moon and stars.

   Across the chest: two small dragons, the axe and the pheasant (symbols of the Emperor's power).

   Under the dragons (left to right): grain (life); water weed (purity); bronze cups (filial piety); fire (cleverness); mountains (enduring strength).

6. When complete, cut out the robe and hang it on a length of bamboo.

Japanese Kimono Designs

Kimonos were worn by all kinds of people, not just those in the royal court. They are held in place by a sash called an 'obi'. Incorporating exquisite embroidery or 'painting with the needle', they were often exhibited as works of art.

Kimono designs often balance images made by people (e.g. geometric shapes, fans, musical instruments) with images from the natural world (e.g. willow and pine trees, leaves, bamboo, birds, butterflies, dragonflies, waves, snowflakes, clouds and flowers).

Approach

1. Draw and cut out a template for a long- or short-sleeved kimono, as in the photograph above.

2. Pencil a design on the template. Include a balance of natural and manufactured motifs, such as flowers with geometric shapes or snowflakes with fans.

3. Draw round the template onto the fabric, using a fabric pen. Then draw in your kimono design, using fabric pens for outlines and fabric crayons for filling in the colours.

4. Put a sheet of paper over the fabric and iron over it to fix the colours.

5. Add touches of gold glitter.

6. Cut out the kimono when the glitter is dry. Two kimono shapes may be stitched together to make a robe for a Japanese puppet.

7. Make an obi in the same way, using a long strip of material.

Note: The obi in the photograph includes images of pine, bamboo and plum – it is called 'The Three Friends' and is considered lucky.

Resources
- Paper for template
- Fabric crayons and felt-tipped pens
- Clothes iron
- Pastel-coloured polycotton
- Fabric glitter pens

Islamic Prayer Rugs

Muslims pray either in the mosque, facing an exquisitely decorated arch called a 'mihrab', or elsewhere, on a prayer rug. The rugs have a central mihrab shape and coloured, patterned borders.

Resources
- White drawing paper
- Felt-tipped pens
- Watercolour paints
- Gold marker pen

Mihrab shapes

Approach

1. Use a pencil and ruler to draw borders around the outside of a rectangular sheet of paper – 1cm, then 2cm, then 1cm in width.

2. Make a symmetrical mihrab-shaped template from scrap paper (see drawings, right). On the drawing paper, draw round the template in the central area and pencil in other divisions such as columns, small arches or a hanging lamp.

3. Paint each area of the design in rich water colours using red, blue, purple, yellow and white.

4. Using felt-tipped pens and a gold marker pen draw decorative patterns in the three borders, and around the mihrab and central area. Islamic motifs include octagons, eight-pointed stars, lozenges, diamonds, stepped and flower patterns.

Islamic Stars

Resources
- Octagon shapes in white card
- Felt-tipped pens, or crayons
- Black marker pen
- Sequins, oddments of foil

Approach

1. Draw lines using a pencil and ruler to link the corner points of a card octagon.

2. Continue to draw lines linking intersecting points, building up a symmetrical star pattern. Many different star shapes can be made.

3. Colour in the pattern symmetrically using red, blue, purple and yellow, leaving some areas white.

4. For crisp outlines, go over ruler lines with black pen.

5. Embellish with eight sequins or foil triangles.

Note: A star or mihrab would make a good motif for a 'Happy Id' card with a verse from the Koran inside.

Inca Geometric Designs

Today's weavings in Peru still use the Incas' geometric square designs and stylised animals, birds, frogs, snakes and fish.

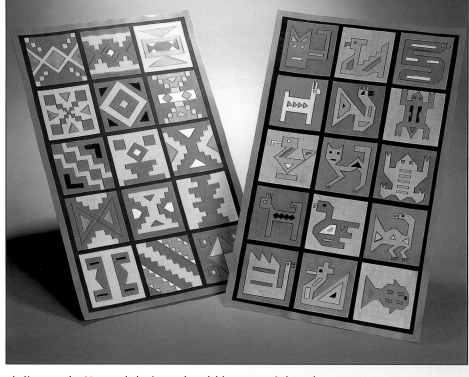

Resources
- 1cm-squared graph paper cut into 10cm squares
- Chalk pastels
- Black graphite pencil
- Fixative
- PVA glue

Approach

1. Choose a geometric or animal motif for each 10cm square and sketch it on rough paper. Geometric designs should be symmetrical and could include zigzags, squares, steps, triangles and diamonds. Natural designs should have straight edges, not curves.

2. Lightly draw the designs on the graph paper, following the lines and including whole and half 1cm squares where possible. Outline firmly with a ruler and pencil.

3. Colour the designs with chalk pastels. Limit the background colours to three so the finished designs can be arranged in rows or diagonal lines of colour.

4. Spray with fixative. Outline each design using a graphite pencil and a ruler.

5. Arrange the squares on backing paper and glue into place.

Peruvian Portrait Pots

Peruvian potters such as the Nazca and Moche brought their pots to life with realistic faces, clothes and beautiful colours.

Resources
- Brown paper
- Black felt-tipped pen
- Wax crayons

Approach

1. Fold the paper in half and draw a pot shape with a recognisable head section. Cut it out and unfold to make a symmetrical pot.

2. Draw a person on the pot in black pen, including details of hat, clothes, face and hair. In the photograph are pots showing, from left to right: person decorated with figures and geometric designs; man with headdress and animal images on the body; Nazca woman holding fruits; and Moche warrior.

3. Colour with wax crayons.

Irish High Cross Bookmarks

The great Celtic stone crosses with their intricate interlaced designs were erected from the eighth to the tenth century. Scripture crosses have panels depicting scenes from biblical stories, saints' lives and stories of good triumphing over evil.

Resources
- White card
- Soft and hard pencils
- Round templates
- Hole punch

Palmette   S-dragon   Triskele

Approach

1. Draw two concentric circles on card. Draw a cross, using a ruler, centrally through the circles. Rub out the central lines and draw four balanced curves instead. Draw a base for the cross.

2. Cut out the cross and then cut out the four curves, starting the cuts with a hole punch.

3. Divide the cross into panels and fill each with rich details. Use a soft pencil to shade some background areas and a hard pencil to emphasise details. Include Celtic patterns (see drawings, above) and scenes from Bible stories, the lives of saints or heroes and animals, or Celtic myths such as Camelot.

Illuminated Letter

Illuminated manuscript books, such as the Book of Kells, are full of Celtic patterns. From the elaborate letters lions spring, monsters gape, warriors march and cats chase mice.

Resources
- Square of card
- Watercolour paints
- Waterproof inks
- Quill feather

Approach

1. Mark out a border on the card and draw a large initial letter centrally, with an animal head on it. In the photograph, the letter 'J' shows a dragon with a human foot disappearing into its jaws.

2. Copy over the pencil lines with a quill dipped in ink. Fill the letter and border with patterns.

3. When the ink is dry, paint with pale water colours. The ink will stop the colours running together.

Self-portrait Drawings

Portraiture has been a popular subject for artists in Western Europe from the earliest carved stone busts of the fourteenth-century sculptor Peter Parler.

Resources
- Good quality drawing paper in soft browns or greys
- Charcoal
- Fixative
- White chalk
- Corrugated card
- Range of soft and hard pencils
- Stand-up mirrors

Approach

1. Study self-portraits by artists such as Rembrandt and Cézanne. Show the children the different marks that can be made with soft and hard pencils, chalk and charcoal. Practise drawing dark and light lines, shading and cross-hatching and rubbing in chalk or charcoal with a finger.

2. Look in the mirror. Notice the shape of the head and chin, the position of the eyes about halfway down the face, and where the nose and ears start and stop. Note how the iris is partly under the upper eyelid. Impress on the children that they should look twice before drawing each feature.

3. Use a soft pencil, held loosely, to lightly sketch in the shape of the face. Keep looking in the mirror. First, draw the eyes, then the mouth, nose and ears, thinking carefully of placement and proportion. The lines should be barely visible, so they can be easily corrected.

4. Define the drawing by shading with soft pencil more heavily around the lower face and the features. Pay particular attention to details on the eyes. Use a hard pencil for fine lines.

5. Add hair with soft pencil and charcoal. Note the direction of hair at the top and sides. Draw in the neck and shoulders, with other details such as freckles, dimples or earrings.

6. Position the subject side-on in good natural light. Notice where light falls on the face and where the shadows are. Rub chalk onto the drawing to highlight one side of the face and charcoal to show light shadows. Use a soft pencil to add shading lines or cross-hatching to the darker areas of shadow.

7. Spray with fixative. Glue on a frame of four strips of corrugated card, painted gold.

Decorated Houses

Approach

Method for Romany Gypsy Wagon (England)

1. Cut the shaded area in the drawing off a shoebox. Mark and cut a stable door at one end of the shoebox.

2. Using felt-tipped pens, decorate the box with traditional patterns (horseshoes, horse heads, flowers, birds, baskets of fruit, scrolls and ribbons).

3. Glue a flat piece of balsa under the box to make a platform outside the door. Decorate with gold side pieces and a zigzag card ladder.

4. Cut a piece of card to make a curving roof and glue in place.

5. Make two large and two small gold card wheels. Tape two pieces of cane under the box for the axles, push on the wheels and hold them on with Plasticine. Glue on two sticks for the horse shafts.

Method for Haida Chief's House (Native American)

1. Invert a white shoebox. Cut out two shallow triangles of card, the bottom edge of which should be the length of the shoebox. Glue the triangles to the front and back of the box to make a roofline.

2. Cut out and glue on three card totem poles, a larger one in the middle. Cut out an oval doorway.

3. Rub all over with brown wax crayon. Use reference books to choose a totem design and decorate the poles and walls. A grizzly bear totem is shown above.

4. Cut a card roof, 3cm longer than the box, fold it in half and glue on twigs. When dry, glue to the box.

Method for Tipi (Native American Plains people)

1. Cut a piece of white card out as in the line drawing (right).

2. Rub brown crayon over the card for a rawhide effect. Mark the semicircular lines, as in the drawing.

3. Draw rows of pattern around the door and the semicircular borders. Fill the central area with warriors, feathers and animals such as deer, bear, buffalo and horses.

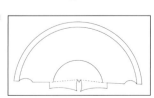

4. Tape the tipi into a cone. Tape sticks inside to project through the smoke hole.

Alternative

Using a rectangular strip of card for the walls and a circular card cone with straw for the roof, make a South African Ndebele mud house (see photograph on page 4).

Buffalo-skin Drawings

Enormous herds of buffalo once roamed the Plains of North America. They were sacred to the nomadic peoples, who depended on them. As well as eating the meat, Native Americans used the skins to make tipis, clothes, shields, bags and containers. Painted buffalo robes were greatly prized and used as clothing or bedding.

Resources
- Neutral-coloured paper
- Felt-tipped pens or crayons
- Brown wax crayons

Approach

1. To make the paper look like rawhide, crumple it, open it out and then rub it all over with the side of a brown wax crayon.

2. Draw the shape of a buffalo skin on the waxed paper and cut it out. Darken the edges by rubbing again with the brown wax crayon.

3. Draw a scene or design on the 'skin'. Shown above is a red and black adaptation of a Sioux design called 'box and border', worn by women. Each part of the design represents an important stage of a woman's life. On the 'skin' below is a battle scene, with horses and warriors, from a Pawnee robe. The children's designs could also record a personal experience, a family occasion or historical event.

Parfleche Containers

These rawhide cases were beautifully painted in geometric designs. Dried buffalo meat was put inside and the edges of the case were folded over and laced up. The case was then hung on a saddle.

Resources
- Rectangle of card
- Leather strips
- Felt-tipped pens
- Hole punch

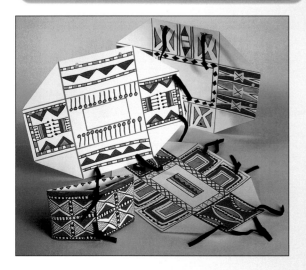

Approach

1. Draw two lines widthways, 8cm in from each edge. Draw another two lines lengthways, 6cm in from each edge. Then cut the four corners off to achieve the shape seen in the photograph.

2. Design and draw geometric patterns within each rectangular section of the card, keeping the design symmetrical. Include diamonds, triangles, ovals, squares, crosses and zigzags. Colour in red, green and black.

3. Punch two holes along the outer edge of each rectangular section, as seen in the photograph. Thread leather strips or ribbon through the holes in two adjacent edges.

4. Fold up the parfleche. First fold lengthways along the drawn lines, and tie the strips. Then fold widthways on the lines and tie up. Keep your treasures inside.

Hopi Ceremonial Drawings

Hopi legends, sacred dances and ceremonial customs have been recorded on sand paintings, rock carvings and pictographs in the cliff dwellings and on cave walls in Arizona, where the Hopi lived many years ago. This drawing is based on a sand painting of the snake legend.

Resources
- Coloured paper (black, red, green, white and shades of brown)
- Brown backing paper
- Felt-tipped pens

Approach

1. Cut out coloured paper circles with the following diameters: red – 30cm; black – 29cm; green – 28cm, white – 27cm; browns – 26cm.

2. Glue the paper circles to the brown background in the order shown in the photograph. Arrange quarter circles of browns as shown.

3. Draw the snake legend in the quadrants. From top left, working clockwise:
   - The Hopi chief gives prayer sticks to his son, to go to the snake people in search of rain
   - The son's boat floats down the Colorado River between the canyon walls
   - The Snake people's priest gives the son a bag of rain-making secrets, a bow and a wife
   - The couple return home with rain blessings falling from the bow and the clouds.

4. Above the circle, draw the sun (the father of all living things), exhaling the breath of life. Below, draw the mouse in the moon, the Hopi equivalent of the 'man in the moon'.

5. Draw rows of canes to the left and right, to show the growth of man and his decline with age.

6. All around the circle, draw symbols of fish, birds, animals, plants, tracks, weather and sacred kivas (underground religious chambers). Use some of the symbols on the right and make up some of your own.

Mexican Papier-mâché Bowls

The patterns on the bowls are taken from Mexican woven rugs and serapes (traditional woven blankets worn by men over one shoulder). A limited number of patterns are combined, including brightly coloured zigzag and diamond patterns and those drawn below.

Approach

1. Cover the mould with cling film.

2. Tear the kitchen paper into pieces and apply a layer over the cling film – this should be wetted, not pasted.

3. Apply four more layers of paper pieces with cellulose paste. Smooth down the paper and allow to dry.

4. Remove the papier-mâché plate from the mould.

5. Design a pattern on a circle of paper. Look at the drawings for ideas. Think carefully about the position of the elements, keeping the design bold and symmetrical and perhaps working with a multiple of four or eight. If necessary, use templates such as diamonds, triangles and circles.

6. With a pencil, copy the design lightly onto the papier-mâché plate. Measure and rule off lines carefully and draw around templates.

7. Paint the design using a medium brush for the background and a fine brush for small areas of pattern. Start painting at the centre and work out to the edges, turning the plate as you work. Use bright primary colours and allow adjacent colours to dry so they do not run.

8. When the paint is dry, go over the pencil lines with a black felt-tipped pen.

Resources
- Large bowl or plate for mould
- Cellulose paste
- Cling film
- Paints, black felt-tipped pen
- White kitchen paper

Body Paintings

Body painting is used to make the body more attractive or to show status or clan membership. It may be used at ceremonial occasions such as for a birth or marriage. Ritual colours are often made using local materials such as stones, plants or coloured clays. These are ground up, mixed with oil or water, and painted on with fingers, twigs or grass brushes.

Resources
- Sugar paper
- Paints, including a range of skin tones
- Sticks, feathers
- Oddments of fabric for clothes
- Plastic boards (for Surma designs)

Approach

Method for Figures

1. Draw a body outline on the paper. Draw around a child for a life-size figure. Paint with skin tones and allow to dry.

2. Paint and decorate the figures as follows:

   - Amerindian girl (left) from the Tembé tribe. Paint on dark red patterns with a finger. Red symbolises life and blood. Traditional patterns are shown below right (a geometric design on the left and a 'jaguar' design on the right).

   - Aboriginal dancer (right) from Australia. Traditional colours are white clay with red or yellow ochre. Paint on white and red circle and line patterns. Make rows of dots with a stick dipped in paint. Glue on feathers.

Method for Surma Designs (below left)

1. Brush white paint over a large plastic board, evenly but not too thickly.

2. Scrape a design out with the fingers. Try an abstract design, an animal skin (giraffe, leopard, zebra), an insect (bee, ladybird), the sun, stars, cobwebs or leaves.

3. Lay brown paper over the design, press very gently and take a print.

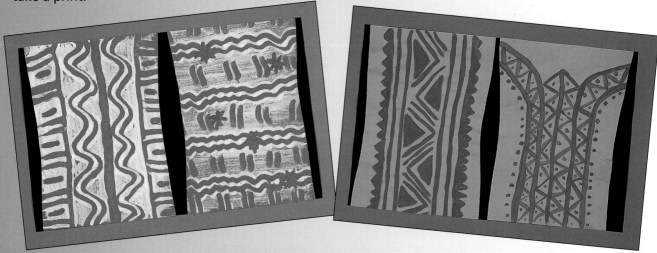

Face Paintings

Faces are decorated for a range of reasons – for beautification, as a means of self-expression, for ceremonial or religious occasions, to show the status of the wearer, or as protection against evil.

Resources
- Sugar paper
- PVA glue
- Range of paints including skin tones
- Feathers, leaves, foils, shells, wool for hair

Approach

1. Draw and cut out a face shape, including ears. Mark the positions of eyes, nose and mouth.

2. Paint the face carefully, using the ideas below. Glue on other decorations such as hair, jewellery and feathers.

Top left: Mexican Huichol face painting to celebrate the maize harvest. Paint yellow, with orange lines for the cornfields and dots for the growing corn. Paint the hair and glue on feathers.

Top centre: Papua New Guinea face, where body decoration is worn for singing and dancing, ceremonies and rituals. Use bright red, blue, yellow and white to paint patterns. Glue on feathers, real leaves and shells if available, for a headdress and silver tusk-shaped earrings.

Top right: Nuba man (African Sudan). Painting is a sign of beauty and strength. Paint with orange and black abstract, zigzag patterns or animal patterns such as giraffe, zebra or leopard.

Bottom left: Surma of Ethiopia, painted for beautification and to show strength in fighting duels. Paint with skin colour and add white stars, circles or geometric patterns. Paint the hair and glue on circular foil earrings.

Bottom centre: Maori woman wearing the traditional spiral tattoo pattern on the mouth and chin. Tattooing was a sign of rank and made women more attractive and men more fierce. Paint the face with skin tones and draw spiral patterns with a felt-tipped pen. Paint the hair. Colour and glue on a patterned headband, and a feather.

Bottom right: Iroquois, Native American, painted for battles, sport and mourning. Paint half yellow and half orange. Add semicircular wheel patterns at the sides and forehead lines. Paint the hair and finish with three feathers.

Aboriginal Desert Patterns

The vast desert lands of central and western Australia are rich in spiritual meaning to the Aboriginal peoples. The lands are covered with a network of paths travelled by the ancestors from the Dreamtime (see page 12).

The events of the Dreamtime are shown in Aboriginal ceremonial sand paintings, made by sprinkling coloured earth onto the soil. Dots, lines and repeated marks are essential features of the art. Dots may represent birds, feathers, sunlight on water, fire, smoke, clouds or rain.

Resources
- White card
- Paints (black, white, yellow and red ochre only)
- Sticks
- Black felt-tipped pen

Approach

1. Draw a shield or boomerang shape on white card and cut it out.

2. Draw a design on scrap paper, using some traditional symbols (below), or making up your own. When you are satisfied with the composition, draw it in pencil on the card.

3. Paint the background areas of the shield first, in either yellow or red. Let these dry before painting in the circles, lines and other patterns you have drawn. Some areas can be left white. Allow to dry.

4. Decorate further with rows or areas of dots printed with a stick or pencil end. Use a different stick for each of the four colours, to keep the colours clean. Small details can be drawn or outlined with black felt-tipped pen.

5. To add a holding band to a shield, cut a strip of card about three-quarters of the width of the shield. Tape it across the centre of the back so that the shield curves.

Camp, waterhole or fire	Adults and children	Water course, lightning, smoke or ancestral path	Boomerang or wind-break	Spears or digging sticks	Fire, smoke, clouds or rain	Tracks made by people or animals

Aboriginal Rarrk Paintings

Cross-hatched patterns on bark paintings, called 'rarrk', are a feature of designs in Arnhem Land, in Australia. The subjects are often animals or images of ancestors from the Dreamtime (see page 12). The background is usually plain. White, red, yellow and black are the main colours. X-ray style pictures showing bones and intestines are also common.

Resources
- Paints (red ochre, yellow, browns and white)
- Painting pencils
- Sticks

Approach

1. Choose a traditional subject such as an Australian animal, bird or fish design, or research an Ancestral Being from Dreamtime stories, such as Yingarna or Nawura. Draw the subject lightly on sugar paper and paint it white. Paint the background in red, yellow or brown and allow to dry.

2. Divide the subject into areas with a ruler to form squares, rectangles or triangles.

3. Fill in each area with patterns of ruled lines, using dry painting pencils. Create patterns of zigzags, diamonds, lines and concentric squares. Some sections can be left white. Others may be thickly coloured in with the painting pencils.

4. Use a fine brush to lightly paint water over the areas that have been coloured in. Keep the brush almost dry.

5. Finish the design by printing dots of paint with a stick, around the outline of the subject. Print dots around the edge for a border.

Polynesian Tapa Design

'Tapa' is a traditional bark cloth made by women in the South Pacific for clothing or religious purposes. Mulberry bark fibres are woven to make a white cloth, which is block printed with black, brown, white and red-brown patterns.

Resources
- 30cm squares of white paper
- Paints (black, brown, beige, red)
- Black background paper
- Rulers and geometric templates
- Polystyrene tile oddments
- Square dowel for printing
- Thick brown marker pen

Approach

1. Choose one or two motifs from those in the photograph right. Note how each is based on a square.

2. Carefully divide up the white paper into quarters or thirds by folding or measuring. The three central squares were folded lengthways into three. The other squares were folded into quarters. Rule pencil lines along the folds.

3. Draw your chosen motifs onto each section of the paper. Use templates and rulers and measure and centralise the designs. Paint the designs carefully, leaving some areas white.

4. Mount the squares on black paper to make a square, leaving a border of black paper visible all round.

5. Make a printing block by gluing four triangles of polystyrene to a 10cm square of card (see drawing, right).

6. Roll the block with white paint and print a repeat pattern around the edge to make an outer border. Print small squares with the square dowel, as an inner border.

7. Outline parts of the pattern with brown pen and a ruler to give crisp outlines to the colours.

Melanesian Kap-kap Ornaments

This popular head ornament is made of white clam shell, incised with concentric circles of pattern. The numbers '4' and '7' feature strongly in the design.

Resources
- Seven round templates of different sizes
- Sugar paper
- Brown paint

Approach

1. Using templates, draw seven concentric circles on the paper and a four-pointed cross in the centre. Mark out one or two of the circular bands into seven segments if desired.

2. Start painting from the centre. Paint the cross, with four little figures in the arms of the cross. Use a fine brush and turn the paper as you work.

3. Paint a different pattern on each band, using repeated dots, semicircles, wavy lines or a capital letter from your name ('E' is shown in the photograph). Finish with the outside band.

Hindu Floor Decorations

Floor decoration is a popular form of everyday folk art in India, especially at festival times.

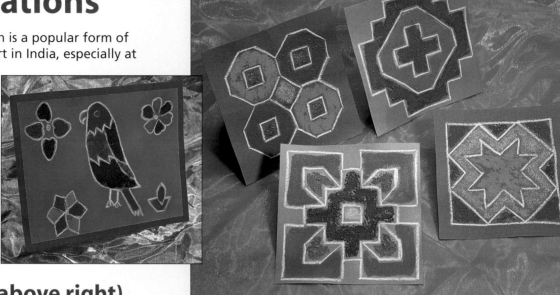

Rangoli (above right)

These are traditionally drawn at the festival of Diwali, to honour the goddess Lakshmi and to welcome the Hindu new year.

Approach

Resources
- Sugar paper
- Coloured powders (sand, ground chalk and clay, powder paints)
- White chalk
- Pegboard
- Graph paper
- Fixative
- Glue

1. Push a fine pencil or nail through a pegboard to make a grid of dots 2cm apart on a square of sugar paper. Grids of 7 by 7, or 8 by 8 work well.

2. Fold a square of graph paper into quarters to show the two axes of symmetry. Design a symmetrical pattern on it, using whole squares and half squares, following the graph paper lines.

3. Copy the pattern you have made onto the grid of dots using white chalk.

4. Coat the central area of the design with glue and sprinkle carefully with one of the coloured powders. Shake off the excess. Repeat with each area of the design, using a range of colours symmetrically.

5. Allow to dry thoroughly, then spray with fixative.

Variation

Parrots, leaves and flowers may be drawn as a welcoming threshold design (above, left).

Alpana (right)

These are traditionally drawn with rice paste to mark births, weddings and festivals such as Basanta, the beginning of spring – when the fields are bright yellow with mustard flowers.

Approach

Resources
- Circle of Perspex
- Brown paper
- Yellow or cream paint
- Paint roller

1. Using a roller, cover the Perspex evenly with yellow or cream paint. Scratch out a pattern which includes flowers, spirals and leaf shapes, with four or eight items round a central point and two axes of symmetry.

2. Place paper lightly on the Perspex and very gently use the roller over it.

3. Remove the paper. Trim when dry and mount on circles of yellow card.

Greek Vase Paintings

Ancient Egyptian art followed strict rules and did not try to show what the world really looks like. A revolution in the history of art came when, by the fifth century BC, Greek artists painted and sculpted what they saw. Their art shows a mastery of movement and expression. They had discovered the method of foreshortening. Natural forms could be painted from the angle at which they were seen – artists dared to paint a foot viewed from the front for the first time.

Approach

1. Look at the shapes of Greek pots and choose one. Fold the paper in half (lengthways for a tall pot, widthways for a wide one). Draw half a pot on the paper and cut it out to make a symmetrical shape. Glue on a pair of identical handles.

2. Paint the design on the pot using good quality, fine brushes. Paint a picture from a Greek story in the centre, such as Daedalus and Icarus, King Midas, or Theseus and the Minotaur.

3. Paint bands of pattern along the top and bottom such as Greek Keys (see below for examples) or palmettes (see page 34). Use black paint on orange pots, orange paint on black pots.

4. When the paint is dry, you may wish to add extra pattern or detail with felt-tipped pens.

5. Display the pots in rows on shelves.

Resources
- Orange-red paper or black paper
- Orange or black paint and felt-tipped pens

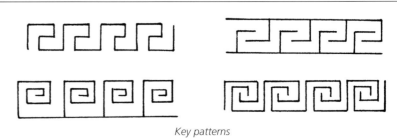

Key patterns

English Watercolour Paintings

The classic English tradition of watercolour painting reached great heights with Thomas Girtin and J M Turner in the eighteenth and nineteenth centuries. Watercolour is excellent for catching quick impressions, but can be used for fine detail, too.

Resources
- Watercolours, watercolour brushes and mixing palette
- Watercolour (or fairly thick) paper
- Large pot of water

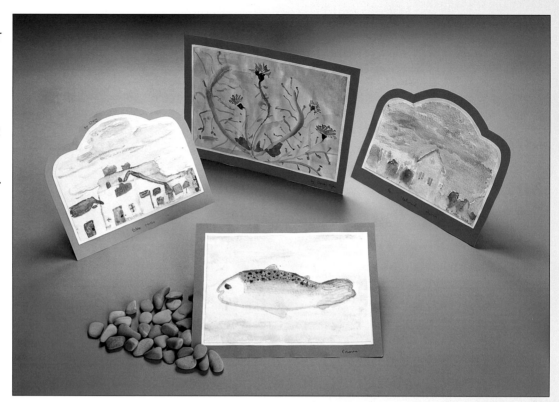

Approach

1. Look closely at watercolour paintings by artists such as J M Turner. Note how the delicacy and transparency of the watercolours capture atmospheric space and light.

2. Show the children how to mix colours in the palette – to lighten a colour add more water; to darken it add more paint. Practise mixing colours and try them out on paper.

3. Choose and observe a subject for painting, such as a still-life, landscape or view from a window. Look carefully at shapes, sizes and proportions. Shown above are two still life paintings (a rainbow trout and cornflowers) and two street scenes. A viewfinder (a rectangular hole in a piece of card) is useful for isolating part of a street scene or landscape.

4. Draw a light pencil outline first, or work directly with paints. Begin by working on large areas of colour, such as sky or water. Use a large brush and work quickly, applying various bands of colour across the paper, depending on the weather effects required. Wet colours will flood into each other and create interesting tones. Some areas of sky can be left white. Some areas can be painted first with water, before adding paint. More colour can be stroked in, wet on wet, and allowed to mingle. Avoid overworking, or the colours become muddy.

5. Use a fine brush for detailed work. Let each colour dry before applying adjacent colour, or they will run together. A little silver poster paint can be mixed with water for a soft sheen (as used on the trout).

Notes:

- Clean brushes between colours and keep the water clean.
- If colours run accidentally, use a dry brush or cotton bud to stop the run.
- Lift excess colour out of wet areas by rolling with a dry brush. A soft tissue can lift wet colour from a sky to create cloud effects.
- Sprinkle rock salt on wet paint for speckled effects such as snow in a sky or texture on a wall. Brush it away when dry. Watercolour over white wax crayon gives good resist effects.

Kenyan Scenes with Printed Borders

Painting on a dyed background captures the warm, bright colours of an African landscape and is well suited for scenes from African tales. Shown above are some typical scenes from the African plains: a giraffe eating from a banana tree; a Maasai warrior with his long plaited hair and spear; a Kikuyu village scene with round mud brick houses and thatched roofs; a herdsman tending his hump-backed cattle.

Approach

1. First, dye the cloth. To do this, paint two colours in random areas on the cloth using large brushes. Let the colours flow together. Allow to dry.

2. Decide on a geometric design. Keep it fairly simple as it will be repeated to make a border. Try zigzags, squares, triangles, diamonds, crosses, arrowheads or a small animal such as a lizard or snake. Prepare a printing block by drawing the design on the polystyrene, using a sharp pencil and pressing quite firmly.

3. Tape a 6cm strip of tape to the back of the block, so it can be picked up with the fingertips.

4. Put a few spoonfuls of black fabric paint on the damp sponge in the tray and spread the paint around so the sponge is saturated. Press the prepared block onto the sponge a few times. Do a test print on paper to check for even coverage. Next, carefully print the border, starting near a corner and repeating the prints close together. Turn the corners, keeping them square. Allow to dry.

5. Design the central scene on paper, then draw it lightly on the cloth in pencil. Paint the silhouettes carefully, using a fine brush and black fabric paint. When it is completely dry, iron to fix the colours.

Notes: If desired, small touches of silver fabric glitter may be added, to highlight details such as jewellery, eyes or weapons. The paintings can also be made on absorbent paper, rather than cloth.

Resources
- White cotton cloth
- Fabric dyes (blue, green, yellow and pink) and black fabric paint
- Smooth polystyrene rectangle 8cm by 4cm
- Small printing tray lined with damp sponge
- Double-sided adhesive tape
- Clothes iron

Navajo Rug Designs

The classic Navajo rug design began with stripes and zigzag motifs, borrowed from basketry. One traditional pattern used five stripes and nine blocks. Red diamonds and bar motifs were borrowed from the Spanish serape. Designs also include aspects of daily life, such as animals, houses and plants, stylised figures and sacred motifs.

Resources

- Paper
- Waterproof inks and fine brushes
- Watercolour paints (black, yellow, grey, browns and red)
- Brown or black backing paper

Approach

1. Look carefully at pictures of Navajo rugs and draw a simple design on a rectangle of paper, using a ruler and pencil. Keep the design balanced and symmetrical with a border, if desired.

2. Paint over the lines with brown or red waterproof ink and a fine brush. The ink will separate the colours and prevent them from running together. Allow to dry.

3. Paint each area of the design with watercolours.

4. Mount on paper. Fringe the borders.

Fulani Celebration Masks

Every year, after a migration in search of pasture, the Fulani of West Africa drive their cattle across the dangerous River Niger back to the villages. Afterwards, the crossing is celebrated with musicians, storytelling and ritual dancers in bright costume wearing rectangular box masks on their heads.

Resources

- White shoebox
- Bright paints
- Black marker pen
- Torn strips of pink and white fabric
- Crêpe-paper tassels
- Silver card

Approach

1. Mark the box into square and rectangular areas.

2. Paint concentric squares or rectangles in each area, allowing adjacent colours to dry so they do not run together. Allow to dry.

3. Use a thick black marker pen to outline the squares.

4. Decorate with streamers of fabric at the back, crêpe-paper tassels along the top and silver card circles for 'eyes'.

Nazca Lines Bleach Paintings

The 2 000 Nazca lines of Peru are one of the world's greatest examples of earth art. Drawn in the desert are enormous birds, geometric shapes, spirals and animals, such as a 180-metre lizard and a 90-metre monkey with a curled tail.

Resources
- Black cloth in variety of cotton materials
- Thick bleach in a flat lid
- Cotton buds

Approach

1. Look at pictures of the Nazca lines. Choose a design and sketch it on paper.

2. Dip a cotton bud in the bleach and copy your drawing onto the cloth. A surprising variety of colours emerge from different fabrics, such as pink, orange, yellow or white. Take care with drips as these will bleach too.

3. Glue the paintings to backing paper in a patchwork arrangement. Draw a geometric border with a ruler and felt-tipped pen.

 This activity requires close supervision. Work in a well-ventilated area, protect all clothing and do not allow children to touch the bleach.

Paper Kimono Dolls

Resources

- Two 10cm paper squares with tiny patterns
- Two strips thin card 5cm by 0.5cm
- 10cm square of plain coloured paper
- White card circle, 2.5cm in diameter
- Black paper

Approach

1. Make the neck by wrapping the thin card strips together, as in the drawing, below right.

2. Glue the square of plain paper to the back of a square of patterned paper. Fold over 1cm of the paper at the top and bottom, so the patterned side of the kimono has plain borders showing.

3. Lay the paper patterned side down and glue the neck centrally, as in the drawing. Next, fold the kimono body as follows: fold in 3cm at the left and right; open out and fold over at a 45° angle on either side of the neck; fold the sides in again along the creases and press firmly.

4. Glue a strip of paper 2cm wide around the body of the kimono, to make an obi (sash).

5. Draw a face on the card circle and glue it to the neck.

6. Cut a hair shape with a slit in it. Slide and glue the head in the slit.

7. Make the sleeves from the remaining patterned square. For furisode (long) sleeves, cut away the shaded areas shown in the drawing and glue to the shoulders. For kosode (short) sleeves, cut away the shaded areas shown in the drawing and glue to the back of the kimono. Fold down the arms or leave them out sideways.

8. These Japanese dolls can be glued to a paper fan decorated with typical Japanese symbols (see page 31 for a list of symbols) or they can be glued to card to make bookmarks.

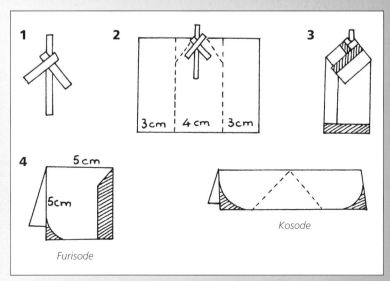

1

2

3cm 4 cm 3cm

3

4

5 cm

5cm

Furisode

Kosode

Simple Origami Projects

Tulips 8cm square of paper	**1.** Fold in half to make a triangle. 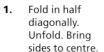	**2.** Fold up corner. 	**3.** Fold up second corner. 	**4.** Draw coloured lines on the flowers. Add green leaves and stems. Glue to card as in the photograph.	
Duck 10cm square of paper	**1.** Fold in half diagonally. Unfold. Bring sides to centre. 	**2.** Turn over. Fold back pointed end. 	**3.** Fold in half. 	**4.** Pull up the neck flap. Press down. Fold over a head. 	**5.** Zigzag fold the tail. 
Gift Basket 15cm square of paper	**1.** Fold in half to make a triangle. 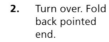	**2.** Fold down top to centre of bottom. Unfold. 	**3.** Fold in sides to align with horizontal crease. 	**4.** Cut along dotted lines in drawing with craft knife. 	**5.** Fold down and glue inner triangles.
Dove or Bird Paper doily or circle of paper, 15cm diameter	**1.** Fold in half twice. 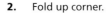	**2.** Fold in two sides to connect the creases. 	**3.** Fold in half. Cut on the line. 	**4.** Fold up flap to make a wing. 	**5.** Turn over. Fold other wing. Fold over a head.
Divided Party Box 30cm square	**1.** Fold in half twice. 	**2.** Take all four corners to the centre. 	**3.** Turn over and repeat. 	**4.** Fold in half twice to make creases. 	**5.** Open pockets. Fill with sweets.

Japanese Floating Dolls

Hina Matsuri, the Japanese Doll or Peach Festival, is on 3 March. It was believed that dolls could drive away misfortune. Paper dolls with the child's name on it were rubbed on the child, then cast in the river to float away with all illnesses. It is customary for girls to be given Hina dolls at birth, to be taken away when they marry. Today, floating dolls may be kept as ornaments. Red is used as it is a symbol of happiness in Japan.

Ten Floating Dolls on a Raft

Resources
- Clay and clay tools
- Lollipop sticks
- Silver pen
- Red and gold paper
- Thick card
- Bamboo

Approach

1. Make ten identical clay cylinders, about 5cm in length. Mark on necks and faces.

2. When the clay is dry, roll a strip of red paper around each cylinder to make the bodies. Glue a little gold sash to each doll and draw on spots with a silver pen.

3. Tie or glue the dolls firmly to a strip of card.

4. Glue lollipop sticks, side by side, on two parallel bamboo sticks to make a little raft for the dolls to float on.

Kimono Dolls in an Origami Boat

Resources
- Clay and clay tools
- Gold glitter glue
- Oddments of cloth
- Red card circle, 15cm in diameter
- Pipe-cleaners

Approach

1. Roll a cylinder of clay about 8cm in length and squeeze a head and neck shape at one end. Impress a face with clay tools. Allow to dry.

2. Wind a pipe-cleaner around the body for arms. Dress the doll in a kimono: glue a square of cloth to the front and back of the doll, and trim to shape.

3. Cut red paper and a paper face, and glue together to make a little paper baby for each doll. Glue in place.

4. To make the boat, fold the circle of card into eight segments and cut away the shaded area shown in the drawing. Open up the card, fold up the eight points and add glitter glue to decorate.

Egyptian Coffins and Mummies

The Ancient Egyptians embalmed or mummified corpses, in the belief that the spirit could live on after death. The dried internal organs were put in clay canopic jars. The mummy was put in a richly decorated coffin. Spells were written in hieroglyphs (see page 10) to protect the spirit. Cats were believed to have the power to grow crops, and were often embalmed. So were other animals such as bulls, dogs, ibises and crocodiles.

Resources
- White card
- Newspaper
- Felt-tipped pens and gold pens
- Adhesive tape
- Plaster bandages

Approach

1. Enlarge the drawing (below) to the size you require. Cut out the lid, base and foot from white card. Fold on the dotted lines.

2. Design the coffin lid. Draw a portrait of the deceased in the top third, giving it a detailed, decorative collar section. Divide up the rest of the lid into more sections and draw colourful gods, symbols and hieroglyphs in each. Draw a pattern all around the folded edges.

3. Glue the snipped sections and bottom corners, bend the edges down and press into a lid shape.

4. Draw a design on the foot casing and fold and glue it to the bottom of the lid.

5. Design the base. Draw hieroglyphs all around it, and patterned edges. Glue the base into shape, as for the lid. Brightly coloured paper or patterns may be added to the interior.

6. To make the mummies, draw an outline of a person, crocodile, cat or other animal on card. Cut it out and check the person fits easily into the coffin. Crunch up small balls of newspaper and tape them to the card outline to make the mummy three-dimensional. Cover with two or three layers of plaster bandage strips (see page 71). Make the shape of feet or arms with bandages. Dry completely and draw on a face.

7. Make canopic jars with card tubes. Add head shapes of a jackal, a falcon, a baboon and a human being. Decorate as above.

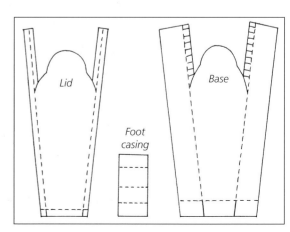

Lid

Base

Foot casing

Egyptian Amulets

The Ancient Egyptians made amulets of gold and semi-precious stones. They were worn as necklaces and bracelets, and were also bandaged up with mummies to protect the spirit in the afterlife. Examples of amulets include the scarab beetle or winged scarab, a symbol of rebirth or creation, and the protective eye of Ra or Wedjat's eye. Children wore fish-shaped amulets, to prevent them from drowning in the Nile.

Resources
- Copper-coloured wire or gold pipe-cleaners
- Gold and silver paint
- Tin foil container
- Clay tools
- Plaster (see page 71) or wax for casts
- Self-hardening dough or clay
- Coloured glass drops or beads

Approach

Method for Clay Amulets

1. Model an amulet (fish or scarab, for example) from clay. Either push in a paper-clip or make a hole through the top for hanging. The turquoise scarab beads on the bracelet in the photograph have a hole through them lengthways. Allow the clay to dry.

2. Paint the clay pieces gold and string them on wire or pipe-cleaners to make a necklace or a bracelet. Incorporate a glass drop, if desired, by crossing wire firmly over it and securing it to the necklace.

Method for Wedjat Eye

1. The Wedjat eye in the photograph was cast in plaster and in wax. To make the casts, press clay smoothly into a tin foil container and scratch the Wedjat symbol on it with a pointed clay tool.

2. Pour in a few spoonfuls of either plaster or melted wax. Rest a bent paper-clip in it for hanging.

3. When the plaster or wax has set, remove the foil and clay and wash the cast.

4. Paint the plaster cast gold.

Amulet Case

Amulets and spells were carried in a tubular case, around the neck. To make an amulet case, glue a card tube between two small foil cake cases and spray with gold paint. Carefully make a hole through the top, so you can put in your amulet or spell. Hang on a thread around your neck.

 Careful supervision is necessary when using hot wax.

Basket-making

Basketry is an ancient technique, practised everywhere. Cheap local materials are used, such as jute in Bangladesh, raffia and leaves in Africa, sisal in Central America and willow in England.

The baskets above are based on red and black baskets from Kalimantan, Indonesia, and a palm-leaf basket from Cameroon.

Black and Red Baskets

Resources
- Red and black card
- Squared paper
- PVA glue

Approach

1. Cut a piece of card to 27cm by 8cm. Fold it in half lengthways. Cut slits every 1.5cm as in the drawing. Open out.

2. On squared paper, design a repeating pattern four squares high.

3. Cut 1.5-cm wide strips of card in a contrasting colour and weave them through the slits, following the square design.

4. Glue down the ends of the strips and bend the weaving into a tube. Staple the ends together.

5. Stand the tube on card, draw round the tube and cut out a circle for the base of the basket. Make half-centimetre cuts all round the bottom of the basket. Bend and glue the snipped edge to the base. Add a handle.

Raffia Embroidered Basket

Resources
- 18cm card circle
- White and coloured raffia

Approach

1. Cut 13 notches into the card circle, as shown in the drawing.

2. Bend up the notches along the dotted line. Rub the base with green crayon to represent palm leaves.

8 cm

3. Tie raffia to the base of a notch and wind it in and out of the notches, building up the rows of weaving to 1cm from the top. Create a gentle slope to the basket as you work.

4. Thread another colour of raffia into a darning needle and stitch it onto the basket to make patterns of crosses, zigzags or lines. Tie off securely and tuck all loose ends behind the weaving.

Note: White raffia can be successfully dyed with any coloured dye. (The use of dye should be supervised.)

Balinese Temple Offerings

Elaborate sculptures made from multicoloured rice dough are made for Hindu festivals and temples. Women carry pyramids of fruit, flowers and rice cookies on their heads to the temples to honour the gods.

Resources

- Salt dough (see page 71)
- Watercolours
- Cocktail sticks
- Oiled baking sheet
- Gold paint
- Garlic press

Approach

Method for Headdress Offering

1. Press a large piece of salt dough onto the oiled baking sheet. Mould it into a flat semicircle. Trim to shape.

2. Mould a face and collar from dough. Stick these to the semicircular base with water.

3. Mould hands, a zigzag crown and blossom. Stick the items on with water.

4. Push dough through a garlic press to make interesting dangling jewellery or hair.

5. Bake (see page 71) and paint brightly. Extra items such as foils or dried flowers may be glued on when dry.

Method for Fruit Pyramid

1. Press a large piece of salt dough onto the oiled baking sheet. Mould it into a flat, rounded oblong for the basket pyramid of fruit. Trim to shape with a knife and smooth well.

2. Mould pieces of dough into a face, shoulders and arm. Attach these with water to the bottom part of the oblong base. Build up rows of eggs, fruits, biscuits and flowers, moulded from dough. Cocktail sticks and dough flowers can be pushed into the top.

3. Bake (see page 71) and paint brightly.

Variation

A popular carved temple image is the Garuda, king of birds. This sacred eagle is often shown carrying the god Vishnu. Cut feathered wing and tail shapes from a 1cm-thick circle of dough. Model a dough head, body, arms and legs for the eagle and stick them on with water. Model a little Vishnu and stick it on to the eagle's shoulders. Add triangles of dough and impressions of feathers. Bake and decorate with stone-coloured watercolour.

Pendants from around the World

Approach

Aztec Quetzalcoatl Chest Ornament (bottom centre)
Roll salt dough (see page 71) into a sausage shape. Curve and arrange it on an oiled baking sheet. Flatten the heads, separate the jaws, and bake. Paint it red all over. When dry, add little dots of turquoise paint using a stick. Cut zigzag card teeth with pinking scissors and glue on.

Native American Kachina Doll (bottom left)
See page 68 for method and materials.

Maori Jade Pendant (bottom right)
Roll and cut a rounded oblong slab of clay. Scratch on details of face, neck, arms and legs so the figure appears to be squatting. Push in a paper-clip for hanging and dry off. Paint it jade green, glue on foil (pearly-side up) for the eyes, and finish with a coat of diluted PVA glue.

Amazonian Feather Pendant (top left)
Cut a background shape from felt. Working from the bottom up, press on a strip of double-sided adhesive tape with a row of colourful feathers on it. Repeat with more rows of taped feathers until the felt is covered. Glue feathers to the top.

Muslim Moon and Star Symbols (top centre)
Cut your chosen symbols from foils and glue them to a piece of felt.

Australian Aborigine Shell Pendant (top right)
Choose a large pearly shell. To make a hole in it for hanging, stick a piece of masking tape to the front and back where the hole is to be located. Put the shell on a thick pad of newspaper and bore a hole through the tape with a hand-drill. Remove the tape and draw a design with a fine black felt-tipped pen. Traditional symbols include Australian animals, fish, insects or hunting implements.

Resources
- Salt dough (see recipe on page 71)
- Feathers, felt
- Raffia or wool for hanging
- Oiled baking sheet
- Clay
- Paints, felt-tipped pens
- Card
- Foils, shells, stick
- PVA glue
- Wood and cork offcuts
- Paper-clips
- Double-sided adhesive tape
- Hand drill
- Pinking scissors

Ritual Necklaces

Approach

Bones Necklace – Andaman Islands, India (bottom left)
Human bones are worn as magical protection against illness and evil forces. Mould clay into bone shapes. Dry off and paint white. Bind the bones tightly to a strip of felt with wire.

Native American Grizzly Bear Cross Necklace (top left)
Bear claws are prized as a symbol of physical and supernatural power. Shape clay into bear claws and round beads. Make holes in them for threading. When the clay is dry, paint the claws and beads, then string them on wire. Make a copper cross pendant out of foil-covered card and hang it centrally.

Sulawesi Chief Crocodile Necklace – Indonesia (top right)
Make the tubular necklace with pieces of bamboo sprayed gold (gold is a symbol of health and good fortune). Thread wire through them, with wooden beads in between. Shape clay into crocodile teeth shapes. Make holes through for threading, and dry off. Paint the teeth and thread them on wire, along with some wooden beads.

Tally Necklace – Papua New Guinea (top centre)
Glue lollipop sticks to two long strips of felt to make the tally necklace. (The length of this represents how many times an Indonesian man has participated in gift exchange ceremonies, and thus how high a status he has.) For the pearl shell crescent, cut a disc of card and cover both sides with silver foil. Bore two holes through the card and thread onto wool. Hang around the neck.

Resources
- Self-hardening clay
- Card
- Lollipop sticks
- Wire
- Foils
- Wooden beads
- Felt
- Bamboo
- Gold spray paint

African Maasai Beadwork

The Maasai of Kenya are traditionally nomads, moving about with their cattle, and their jewellery is a work of art that can be carried when the community moves. Women of marriageable age wear heavy necklaces and earrings made of thousands of glass beads sewn into elaborate ornaments. The warriors also wear jewellery, and particularly treasure arm and leg bands which are made for them as a sign of love. Women's heads are shaved in line with ideals of feminine beauty. The geometric bead patterns often carry significant messages.

Collar

Resources
- Wood offcuts
- Silver foil
- White card
- Ribbon
- Coloured paper
- Coloured drinking straws
- Felt-tipped pens
- Hole punch
- Beads

Approach

1. Glue wood offcuts together to make a head with neck, shoulders and facial features.

2. Measure across the shoulders and cut from card a circle shape with a central protruding 'apron', about the same size. Cut a central hole, and a slit at the back, so the collar fits around the neck (see drawing).

3. Draw concentric pencil rings on the collar, using round templates. Colour the collar brightly with bands of colour. Draw geometric patterns on the 'apron' section.

4. Measure and cut a card neckband, headband and earrings, and decorate lavishly with colour, beads and silver-foil triangles. The earrings and head decoration can be cut from a small folded rectangle of card. Glue everything in place.

5. Punch lots of holes in coloured paper and stick the coloured paper dots around the edge of the collar.

6. Decorate further with strings of beads, ribbons and pieces of drinking straw.

West African Gold Circles

Ashanti Discs

Early European visitors to the Ashanti royal court in Ghana were astounded by the dazzling display of gold jewellery worn against brilliant fabrics. The traditional Ashanti gold discs, added to necklaces and other jewellery, were highly patterned and incised.

Resources
- Self-hardening clay
- Clay tools
- Gold spray paint
- Gold foil
- Gold wire or thread

Approach

1. Roll out a slab of clay and cut it into a circle, using a template.

2. Make patterns by impressing with clay tools and other items, such as square and round sticks, nails or seeds. Try concentric rings of dots, squares or lines, crosses, an animal such as a lizard, snake or insect, cross-hatching or grid patterns with further patterns inside the grid.

3. Make a hole through the disc so that it can be strung.

4. When the clay is dry, spray with gold paint.

5. For the round gold beads, crumple balls of foil smoothly. Thread them by pushing a needle straight through the foil. The balls can also be flattened into discs.

Ibo Anklets

These extremely heavy, but prestigious, anklets were traditionally worn by Nigerian women from adolescence all through their life. They could be gold, copper or brass and were decorated with intricate designs of punched dots.

Resources
- Self-hardening clay
- Gold paint
- Clay tools

Approach

1. Cut a circular slab for the base and a long rectangle of clay for the ankle section. Curve the rectangle into a tube. Attach it to the base with slip (see page 71).

2. Draw your design on the clay. Begin by impressing some outlines of lines and circles, keeping the design symmetrical. Fill in the outlines with rows of impressed dots. Add border patterns or any other details you wish.

3. Allow to dry before spraying with gold paint.

Monster Masks from Southeast Asia

Southeast Asia has a rich repertoire of carved wooden masks of demons, monsters and dragons, used for dramatic dance and the narration of tales such as the Hindu epic, the Ramayana.

Approach

1. Draw a face shape on the card, 20cm wide, with horns, crown or headdress. The peacock mask of Sri Lanka, (bottom left), has two side pieces glued into place. Cut out the mask.

2. Mark and cut out eyeholes.

3. Mark out in pencil the main areas of colour, for example the mouth, teeth, nostrils and tongue. Colour the areas with thick crayons and pastels, leaving black card around them.

4. Use a stick or fingernail to scratch lines and patterns out of the coloured areas, such as feathers on the peacock mask or teeth on the dragon mask (top right).

5. Embellish with glitter, sequins or fur.

6. Attach to a band of card cut to fit the wearer's head.

Maori Ancestral Carvings

Intricate Maori wooden carvings adorned the wooden walls of the meeting house, the heart of cultural life. The carvings tell stories of ancestral figures who are shown as strong and powerful with tattoo-like markings, sometimes with a projecting tongue or holding a green-stone club.

Approach

1. Roll a slab of clay 1.5cm thick. Cut an oval for a head or a rectangle for a house post shape.

2. Model prominent features (tongue, ears, nose) in clay and attach them with slip (see page 71). Cut away eyeholes if a mask effect is desired.

3. Scratch lines on the post to outline a head and body shape. Fill in the design with rows of lines, spirals and other impressed patterns. Make a hole for hanging.

4. Dry the posts flat and the faces over a stick for a convex shape. For a wood effect, paint with brown watercolours.

5. When dry, paint with diluted PVA glue for a gloss finish.

Aboriginal Tiwi-style Sculptures

For the Tiwi islanders off northern Australia, the Pukumani burial ceremony is central to their traditional art. Funeral poles are carved from wood, painted and used to mark graves. The Tiwi see the poles as representing aspects of the life of the deceased. The Pukumani figures are based on the Pukumani pole but have large heads and a 'window' in the body.

Pukumani Figures

Resources
- Plastic bottles
- Plaster bandages (see page 71)
- Bowl of water
- Felt-tipped pens

Approach

1. Make each figure from two plastic bottles, a larger one for the body and a smaller one inverted for the head. Cut and tape the bottle to the right proportions.

2. Cut a window right through the body section.

3. Make the arms from rolled pieces of plastic bottle and tape them in place.

4. Cover the figure with three layers of plaster bandage strips 10cm long (see page 71). Take the strips through the 'window' and smooth the surface well. Dry off completely.

5. Decorate with felt-tipped pens. Traditional patterns are stripes, diagonals, ladders and cross-hatching.

Pukumani Poles

Resources
- Recyclable materials (plastic bottles, lids, cardboard tubes of varying sizes)
- Cellulose paste
- Paints
- Newspaper pieces 4cm by 5cm
- Felt-tipped pens

Approach

1. Make a pole 'figure' by taping together lengths of tubes, lids and bottles. Add a 'head' piece at the top.

2. Cut windows or sections out of some of the figures, using scissors. (An adult can assist using a craft knife if necessary.)

3. Cover the figure with three layers of pasted newspaper pieces, smoothing well to give a good painting surface.

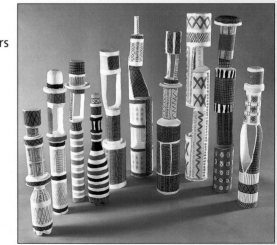

4. When the figure is completely dry, paint it white.

5. Create a design of stripes, large squares or wide bands to fit the pole. Pencil the design on the pole. Paint the marked areas with colour using yellows, reds, black and brown. Leave some areas white.

6. When the paint is dry, use felt-tipped pens in the same range of colours to draw more details onto the painted lines and shapes.

Celtic Heads

The Celts inhabited much of Western Europe before the Roman Conquest. As well as erecting massive hill forts and sacred sites, they had a lively tradition of sculpture and metal-working in which heads are a recurring theme. It was believed the soul lived in the head, and enemy heads taken in battle gave power to the owner. Celtic faces are usually made to look fierce with staring eyes, a droopy moustache, a stiff backswept hairstyle and a beard of spirals.

Resources
- Self-hardening clay
- Silver spray paint, chalk, green paint
- Wire
- Clay tools
- PVA glue
- Brown shoepolish

Approach

Square Slab (from a French shrine, Egremont)

1. Roll and cut a square clay slab. Roll and flatten four balls of clay for the heads. Stick in place with slip.

2. Scratch details of two female faces at the top and two male underneath. Model clay into noses and mouths and attach with slip. Scratch out headdresses, moustaches and eyes.

3. When dry, rub on white chalk with a finger.

Tall Pillar (from Entremont Temple, France)

1. Bang a piece of clay on a table on all sides to make a cuboid.

2. Bend wire into a head shape and impress 12 heads on the pillar. Finish as above for the square slab.

Round Slab (from a silver horse harness, Italy)

1. Roll and cut a 12cm round slab of clay. Stick a small circle of clay centrally with slip (see page 71).

2. Roll and flatten nine balls of clay for the heads. Stick in place and impress the faces' features and hair.

3. Scratch a triskele in the centre, a common Celtic motif with three elements (see page 34).

4. When dry, spray with silver paint.

Three Faces Slab (from a three-headed god on a French terracotta vase)

1. Roll out and cut a square clay slab.

2. Model three faces on it, one facing forward and one in profile on each side. Model raised features with clay oddments and attach with slip. Scratch out details such as spirals for the hair and beard.

3. When dry, brush with diluted PVA for a gloss finish.

Pillar with Head (from an Irish bowl – this represents the nailing of an enemy head to a door post.)

1. Make a pillar, as above. Attach a ball of clay to the top.

2. Incise features and hair on the face and a square pattern on the pillar. Allow to dry.

3. Rub with brown shoe polish and watery green paint.

Mexican Folk Art

All Souls Day, 2 November, is a day of prayer for the dead. In Mexico, shrines are built to honour departed relatives. Biscuits and cakes in the shapes of skulls and coffins are made. Cemeteries are decorated with papier-mâché, life-sized, dressed-up skeletons.

Resources
- Self-hardening clay
- Paint, felt-tipped pens
- PVA glue
- Clay tools
- Nightlight

Approach

Skulls

1. Mould and press a ball of clay into a skull shape. Poke in fingers for eye sockets, press a nose indentation and scratch the shape of teeth.

2. Dry off and paint.

Slab (centre) – this shows three skeletons enjoying a 'Day of the Dead' feast.

1. Roll out an oblong slab with a rounded top. Model three figures in clay and stick them to the slab with slip (see page 71). Add a clay table and three bowls. Scratch out patterns and facial features.

2. When dry, paint all over with white paint.

3. Dry off and draw bones and other details with felt-tipped pens.

Friendship Circle (bottom right) symbolising cooperation and understanding

1. Attach a ball of clay to the centre of a round clay slab. Push in a nightlight.

2. Make five small tubular figures. Attach them with slip around the base facing inwards. Join the figures with strips of clay for arms. Mark on facial features.

3. Allow to dry, then coat with diluted PVA glue.

Candleholder (left in photograph above)

1. Make an inverted thumb pot for the base by pushing a thumb into a ball of clay. Flatten the bottom of the thumb pot. Attach a thick piece of clay vertically for the main support.

2. When this is leather hard, roll and attach two sausage shapes, one at each side. Model and attach a little person, birds or flowers. Scratch out any patterns you wish. Make a hole in each arm of the figure so little clay bells can be suspended inside.

3. Allow to dry before painting.

Skeleton Decoration

Resources
- Black plastic bin liners
- Silver marker pen
- Newspapers
- Double-sided adhesive tape
- Black and white card
- Oddments for decoration

Approach

1. Stuff newspapers into a black bin liner. Make a head and body shape by tying at the neck and waist. Tape on plastic strips for arms and legs, or trousers.

2. Cut hands and feet from black card. Draw bones on these with a silver marker pen and tape in place.

3. Cut a skull, and arm and leg bones from white card. Tape on with double-sided adhesive tape.

4. Decorate as extravagantly as you wish. For the patterns on the dress, see page 39.

Native American Totems

Peoples on the Northwest American coast, cut off from the rest of the continent by the Rocky Mountains, developed a unique culture and complex society, based on animal ancestors. The spirit powers of the ancestors, such as the raven, bear or beaver, were associated with heroic stories. All people sharing the same animal totem would welcome and protect each other.

Totem poles also showed the status of families by recording family trees. The design would incorporate ancestor figures, crests, mythical or historical events, marriage alliances and family occasions.

Felt Collage Totem

Approach

Resources
- Pieces of felt (black, yellow, red and white)
- Strip of backing cloth
- PVA glue

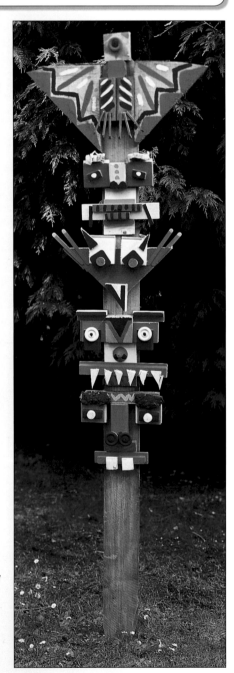

1. Draw and cut out a mixture of animal-head shapes from felt. In the photograph (left), from the top, are the thunderbird (great spirit), the killer whale, the eagle, the bear, the raven (creator and trickster) and the beaver.

2. Glue on facial details in contrasting colours of felt (beaks, eyes, teeth, nostrils and so on).

3. Glue or stitch all the heads in a column on the backing cloth. Cut a repeat pattern from felt oddments and glue it down the long sides.

4. Fringe the edges and glue on a decorative bottom strip. Add a little fabric glitter to highlight details, if desired.

Wooden Totem Pole

Resources
- Long wooden pole
- Range of wooden offcuts in different shapes
- Outdoor varnish
- Wood glue
- Paints

Approach

1. Each child can make an animal-human ancestor face by gluing together wooden shapes and offcuts.

2. Highlight details on the faces with red and black paint, plus a little yellow and green.

3. Glue or screw the faces, one underneath the other, on the wooden pole, with the thunderbird at the top.

4. For outdoor use, coat with two coats of outdoor varnish.

Native American Hangings

Dream Catcher

The dream catcher of the woodland peoples was hung near an open window. It was thought that good dreams know the way through the web and slip through the hole in the centre, so they can be dreamed again. Bad dreams do not know the secret of the web, so get caught and burn off in the morning sun.

Resources
- Plastic hoop (the rim of a container)
- Coloured plastic mesh fruit bag
- 1cm strips of suede or felt
- Beads, feathers and wool
- PVA glue

Approach

1. Put the hoop in the mesh bag. Centralise it, so the bag's join is in the middle of the hoop. Tie the mesh tightly underneath, so it will not move.

2. Wind strips of suede or felt around the hoop, through both layers of mesh, until the hoop is neatly covered. Start and join strips with a little glue.

3. Remove the tie underneath and carefully cut off all the mesh ends at the back, leaving the front intact.

4. Tie on a loop for hanging and double strands of wool at the bottom and sides. Thread beads to the ends of the wool and glue on feathers to finish.

Mandella Shield

The traditional Native American Mandella was hung in a tipi to bring health, happiness and prosperity.

Resources
- Plastic hoop (as above)
- 10cm squares cut from a roll of cotton wool
- Oddments of fur, feathers, wool and beads
- PVA glue
- 1cm strips of suede or felt

Approach

1. Wind suede strips round the hoop, as above.

2. Glue a cross of two suede strips across the hoop and a suede loop for hanging. Glue a circle of fur in the centre.

3. Tie on four double strands of wool at the bottom. Roll the cotton wool squares around each double strand (secured with glue) to make hanging tube shapes.

4. Thread beads onto the end of each strand. Glue on feathers.

Kachina Dolls

To the Native American Hopi and Zuni, the Kachinas are nature spirits from the past, who taught people how to live good, peaceful lives. The dolls educate the children about their heritage.

Resources
- Small wooden offcuts
- Paints
- Oddments of cloth, feathers and card
- Wood glue
- PVA glue

Approach

1. Glue the offcuts together to make a human-shaped figure. Paint when dry.

2. Decide on details of headdress, clothes and carried items. Draw them on card, cut out and glue on the figure. Shown left (from left to right) are: lightning Kachina with lightning bolts on the headdress; owl Kachina holding a bow and arrow; maize spirit Kachina, carrying corn.

Tribal African Dolls

African tribal dolls are related to various social customs and beliefs. The dolls in the photograph below are based on traditional dolls: two tall Ashanti (Ghana) wooden dolls, one with a round head and one rectangular; one Namji (Cameroon) carved geometric doll with coloured bead necklaces; two Sotho (South Africa) clay dolls, covered with bands of beads and a beaded skirt.

Resources
- Wooden dolls: Wood offcuts, wood glue, lollipop sticks, felt-tipped pens, beads, straws, shells
- Clay dolls: Clay, flowerpot, cling film, raffia, beads, felt, paint

WOODEN DOLLS: Select wood offcuts and lay them on the work surface in a doll shape. Glue the pieces together so the doll can stand up (if necessary, use masking tape as a temporary fixing). Draw felt-tipped pen faces. Make necklaces for the Namji doll (left, centre) with beads, cowry shells and straw.

CLAY DOLLS: Cover a flowerpot with cling film. Roll a circle of clay and lay it over the flowerpot. Press and smooth the clay into a dome shape and cut off the excess. Mark out a face. Impress lines for rows of beading. Remove the flowerpot and make holes around the bottom edge of the clay, 1cm apart.

When the clay is dry, paint the 'beaded' hair and body brightly. Tie coloured raffia and beads through the holes to make a skirt. For the arms, string a few beads onto 1-centimetre squares of felt. Glue the felt to the sides.

African Geometric Masks

African masks are worn for entertainment, for celebrations and ceremonies, or for protection against evil spirits.

Resources
- Card circles
- Corners cut from a carton
- Plaster bandages (see page 71)
- Foam oddments
- Card tubes
- Black and red paints
- Fur or crêpe paper
- PVA glue

Approach

1. Look at photographs of African masks and choose a round or rectangular shape. Use a card circle or a carton corner glued to a prism shape.

2. Cut out eyeholes 6cm apart and mark the position of any raised features such as the nose, lips or eyebrows.

3. Cut raised features from foam or card pieces and glue them in place. Tubular eyes (thought to represent ancestors) are a feature of some masks.

4. Cover the mask with pieces of plaster bandage (see page 71), smoothing them over all the raised features and around the eye holes. (Layers of paper may be used as an alternative to plaster bandages.)

5. Paint the masks with typical African geometric shapes such as lines, circles and triangles.

6. Glue on strips of fur or crêpe paper for hair, if required.

African Animal Masks

Stylised animal masks make the wearer strong and give the wearer the powers of the animal. Some masks represent animal ancestors.

Resources
- Black card
- White papers (cartridge, crêpe, tissue, doily)
- PVA glue

Approach

1. Draw the shape of your chosen mask on black card and cut it out. Shown left are: swordfish (New Guinea), antelope (Congo), bird (Mali), elephant (Cameroon) and hawk (Burkina Faso).

2. Measure and cut out the eye holes.

3. Decorate the mask with a range of white papers to create a three-dimensional effect. Show the children how to roll a square of cartridge paper into a tube (for lips, noses, eyebrows) and how to roll paper strips into loops for raised eyes or mouths.

4. Add patterns of zigzags, spots or diamonds cut from paper or torn tissue pieces for a soft, shaded effect.

5. Glue the mask to a band of sugar paper to fit the wearer's head.

Guatemalan Kite

The Cachiquel peoples of Guatemala make giant kites up to 10m across. The pattern grows from the centre as rings of elaborate designs, sometimes with butterflies, flowers and birds. The kites are carried in procession to hilltop ceremonies on 1 November, All Saints' Day, and launched into the wind.

Resources
- Circle of backing paper, 1m in diameter
- Coloured papers and foils
- Crêpe paper
- String

Approach

1. Mark the centre of the circle. From this point, draw six or more circles of different diameters, using a pencil and string.

2. Build up rings of brightly coloured patterns and textures. Add loops, cones, fringes and zigzags.

3. Cut out little paper birds, butterflies or flowers. Glue these on.

4. Add a crêpe paper fringe round the edge.

Note: If you want to launch your kite, glue it to a framework of four lightweight garden canes tied together at the centre.

Japanese Carp Kites

Fish, birds and insects are typical designs on kites flown at festivals and ceremonies in Asia. In Japan, a carp is a symbol of long life, strength and perseverance – qualities the Japanese admire in boys. On Boys' Day, 5 May, the celebrations include flying windsocks painted as carp.

Resources
- Two sheets tissue paper
- 1m bamboo stick
- Poster paints
- Tissue paper circles in two colours
- Flexible wire
- Glitter, foil, string

Approach

1. Staple two sheets of tissue paper together at the four corners. Draw a large fish on the top sheet of tissue paper, giving it a wide mouth and dorsal fin. Cut it out through the two layers.

2. Glue the two pieces together along the top and bottom edges.

3. Decorate the top piece with scales, gluing folded tissue-paper circles on in rows.

4. Paint on scale patterns between and over the tissue circles. Add other lightweight decoration, such as glitter, gold paint or foil shapes.

5. Bend wire into a loop to fit the carp's mouth, keep it in place by gluing and folding the edges of the paper mouth over it.

6. Tie coloured string to either side of the mouth. Tie the string's end to the bamboo stick. Run with the fish, holding it up into the wind.

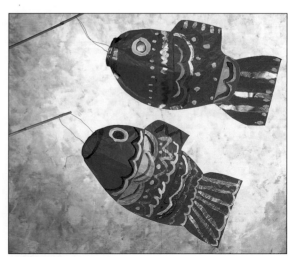

Recipes and Rules

Salt Dough Recipe

1. Mix together until pliable:
   300g plain flour
   300g salt
   1 tablespoon of cooking oil
   200ml water (or a little more if necessary)

2. Knead on a floured board until smooth and elastic.

3. Bake small items for 10–20 minutes on an oiled baking tray at 180°C (350°F), gas mark 4. Leave larger items to cook overnight at 110°C (230°F), below gas mark 1. If the inside is still slightly soft after cooking, leave the work to dry in the air.

Note: Salt dough expands slightly after baking, so if you want to hang up your work make a good-sized hole at the top (or push in a paper-clip). Colour can be added in the mixing water if desired.

Making and Using Slip

1. To make slip, put a few small pieces of clay into a paint pot, add a little water and stir to a creamy consistency.

2. Scratch both surfaces that are to be joined and paint the slip onto them.

3. Gently press the two surfaces together until they bond.

Mixing Plaster

1. Cover the floor and worksurfaces with newspaper.

2. Fill a plastic bucket with water, ready for washing hands and spoons.

3. Make sure your mould or design is ready, as plaster sets in 5–15 minutes.

4. Half fill a plastic bowl with water and sprinkle in plaster until it starts to build up above the surface of the water. Keep adding plaster to empty areas of water, and leave for one minute. As an approximate guide, three cups of water need five cups of plaster.

5. Stir the plaster vigorously with your hand under the water, to eliminate lumps and bubbles. Look at your hand as a test: if the skin colour can be seen, the mixture is a little too thin.

Note: Use only plastic bowls or buckets for mixing. Always add plaster to water, never the other way round. Never pour plaster down a sink.

Using Plaster Bandages

1. Cover the floor and worksurfaces with newspaper.

2. Cut up the bandages into pieces (5cm strips are a good size for smaller items, while bigger items may need pieces about 10cm long). Put the strips in a dry box. If you need more later, use dry hands to cut more strips.

3. Prepare a shallow bowl of water. Dip each piece of plaster briefly into the water. Hold it at the sides as flat as possible, to prevent creasing. Apply it to the item to be covered and smooth with a finger.

4. Cover the required article with at least two or three layers of plaster strips, smoothing it well into crevices and round corners.

Note: The finished, dry plaster can be lightly painted as on page 69. It gives a good surface for felt-tipped pens, as on pages 54 and 63. Materials such as papers, feathers or fabrics can also be glued to it.

Asian Felt (page 8)